A NATURALIST'S GUIDE TO THE HIDDEN WORLD
OF PACIFIC NORTHWEST DUNES

A NATURALIST'S GUIDE TO THE HIDDEN WORLD OF PACIFIC NORTHWEST DUNES

George Poinar Jr.

Oregon State University Press   Corvallis

Library of Congress Cataloging-in-Publication Data

Names: Poinar, George O.
Title: A naturalist's guide to the hidden world of Pacific Northwest dunes /
    George Poinar Jr.
Description: Corvallis : Oregon State University Press, 2016. | Includes
    bibliographical references and index.
Identifiers: LCCN 2015049158 | ISBN 9780870718540 (original trade pbk. :
    alk. paper)
Subjects: LCSH: Sand dune ecology_Northwest, Pacific. | Ecology—Northwest,
    Pacific. | Seashore plants_Northwest, Pacific.
Classification: LCC QH541.5.S26 P65 2016 | DDC 577.5/83—dc23
LC record available at http://lccn.loc.gov/2015049158

♾ This paper meets the requirements of ANSI/NISO Z39.48-1992 (Permanence of Paper).

First published in 2016 by Oregon State University Press

Printed in China

Oregon State University Press
121 The Valley Library
Corvallis OR 97331-4501
541-737-3166 • fax 541-737-3170
www.osupress.oregonstate.edu

CONTENTS

PREFACE

This book had its beginnings with my first visit to the Pacific Ocean in southern California in 1962. After finishing graduate studies at Cornell, I took a position at UC Riverside, and when inland summer temperatures reached over 100°F, I couldn't wait to get to the coast for relief. Walking through the dunes reminded me of family outings along the Eastern Seaboard as a boy. Even then I was fascinated by the plants that grew close to the sea. Repeated trips to the California shores renewed this latent interest, and once I had acquired a background in entomology, botany, plant pathology, and mycology, I was ready to investigate the plants and insects that existed along the Pacific coast. I visited beaches from San Diego north to Morro Bay, Carmel, and Monterey Bay and also examined dune insects on Santa Cruz Island. My first publication on coastal insects dealt with an extensive infestation of kelp flies on Solana Beach in southern California.

Accepting a faculty position at UC Berkeley in 1965 provided an opportunity to shift my dune studies to northern California, starting with coastal life forms around the Marine Laboratory at Bodega Bay. Excursions from the Bay Area to Point Reyes, Fort Bragg, Eureka, and Crescent City in the northern part of the state provided unique samples of dune and strand life. During this period, I had opportunities to visit beaches in tropical and temperate regions around the world and compare their flora and fauna with that of the Pacific coast. I also acquired some expertise in insect pathology and parasitology, which allowed me to further explore these topics in the dune environment.

Finally, acquiring a summer home in Waldport, Oregon, gave me a chance to analyze life farther north along the shores of Oregon and Washington. From here I wrote papers on fascinating dune associations such as a little wasp parasite of dune ants, nematode parasites of carpenter ants and intertidal shore bugs, sawflies feeding on springbank clover, and rare beetles feeding on thimbleberries. Photography was always a keen hobby, and I loved taking pictures of coastal plants and animals, some of which are presented in this book.

ACKNOWLEDGMENTS

This book would never have been written without the love, support, and encouragement of my dear wife, Roberta. Together we made countless excursions along the Pacific coast and spent numerous hours discussing the various types of life found in strand and dune habitats.

I would like to thank the following people for their assistance in identifying various dune biota: Donald Bright, John W. Brown, Daniel Burckhardt, Kenton Chambers, Donald Davis, Julian P. Donahue, John Doyen, Raymond Gagne, Dick Goeden, Pete Haggard, Richard Halse, Paul Hammond, John Heppner, Ron Hodges, Thomas Horton, Tom Kaye, Dick Korf, Jerry Krantz, James LaBonte, the late Jack Lattin, Andrei Legalov, Chuck Meissner, Jeff Miller, Andy Moldenke, Alfred Newton, Allen Norrbom, Barry O'Connor, Gary Parsons, Jerry Powell, the late Frank Radovsky, D. Christopher Rogers, Dana Ross, Barry Roth, Lynn Royce, Scott Shaw, David Smith, Jeffrey Stone, Margaret Thayer, Don Thomas, David J. Voegtlin, Richard Wescott, Margriet Wetherwax, David Wiesemann, Barbara Wilson, Richard Worth, and Kazunori Yoshizawa. I would also like to thank Emily Wirtz for supplying the photo of the Oregon silverspot butterfly and Hisatomo Taki for providing the photo of the mosquito with an attached orchid pollinium.

I am also grateful to the following people who introduced me to specific dune localities or provided other courtesies: Ralph Berry, Alex Brown, Pete Haggard, Andrea Pickart, David Schlesinger, the late Alfred Wiedemann, and my children and grandchildren, whose many questions I hope may now be answered, at least in part, in this work.

INTRODUCTION

Rhythmic tides with perpetually moving waves, far horizons, incomparable sunsets, shifting sands, and unique life forms are some of the reasons we are attracted to the sea. In all seasons, the sun and waves arouse a carefree excitement and joy, a temporary freedom from the mundane activities of fellow earthlings. Respect along with awe and fear are always with me when I hike along the strand with only the shrieking gulls and my dog as companions.

The pulse of the tides and the different types of shore provide unique habitats for a variety of coastal organisms that live nowhere else. Calendars can be set by the running of grunion, the nesting of snowy plovers, the passing of migrating birds, the birth of harbor seals, the flight of dragonflies, and the bellowing of elk. Plants mark the season with blooms, fruit, seedpods, and falling leaves. These events, often unnoticed by visitors, are the elements that make a trip to the coast an educational, fun adventure for all ages and a unique experience to remember in years to come.

When we peer over the windswept strand and dunes, the scene appears bleak and desolate. Many of the organisms that call this home are hidden. Some are diurnal, but others lie buried or concealed under driftwood and rocks during the day and appear only at night. However, clues to the existence of insects dot the sand every morning. Minute impressions appear out of nowhere, move in straight or circular paths, and suddenly halt. The makers might well have come from space, had a walkabout, and then left the earth unseen. I encourage readers to leave their footprints upon the sands as they explore the intricacies of coastal life.

Plants are the most important component of terrestrial habitats and, being at the base of the food chain, are the primary nutritional source for nearly every herbivore and the indirect food source for the carnivores that prey on the herbivores. In the world today, the vast majority of herbivores are insects, which consume far more vegetation in most ecosystems than all other animals combined. Insects play important roles as herbivores, carnivores, and pollinators in the plant communities we will examine on the strand and dunes along the Pacific coast.

This book is a beginning guide for nature lovers, whether naturalists, hikers, or beachcombers, who want to learn more about the plants and their associates along the Pacific coast. These relationships are discussed under individual plants that occur in the strand and dunes. While many life forms of these communities are still unknown, those presented provide an idea of the complexity of life associated with coastal plants. One could spend a lifetime studying just one dune plant and even then would probably never fully discover all the different associated life forms, including the microbes, or comprehend how they all are interwoven.

This book covers plant communities on the Washington, Oregon, and California coastal strand and dunes. These ecosystems are the result of thousands of years of plate tectonics, glaciation, ocean currents, and wind and water erosion. While some organisms occur along the entire coastline, different physical and climatic conditions result in different biota occurring at various locations and during different seasons. The appearance of the Pacific coast changes depending on one's location. For example, in northern Washington, plants have to adapt to pebble beaches, while in southern Washington, Oregon, and northern California, sand dunes are common but are interspersed with cliffs, bluffs, and forests. In northern California the four major dune systems (Lake Earl, Humboldt Bay, Ten Mile, and Manchester) all have unique features, which differ from those of the arid coastal systems in the central and southern portions of the state.

Starting with the kelp and driftwood communities on the strand, we will walk inland, stopping to examine different dune plant communities, most with their own unique set of herbivores, predators, parasites, pathogens, and symbionts. We will then continue past the foredunes, traversing hollows, ridges, and deflation plains as we move inland toward the back dunes.

Most of the plants included are native to the Pacific Northwest coast unless otherwise indicated. Some introduced types that are now well established in dune systems, such as marram grass, have been added. Many dune plants have several common names, but only the most popular one has been selected. Plant scientific names can vary depending on the source, but for the most part, I used the latest edition of *The Jepson Manual* as a reference. Regarding insects and other invertebrates, the size of the immatures varies considerably since they range from hatchlings to mature forms. The adult insects also vary in size, depending on their sex, health, host plant, geographic location, and genetic strain. For simplicity, I used the following terms for the measurements of eggs, mature larvae, and adults: microscopic = under 1 mm; small = 1–10 mm; midsized = 10–20 mm; large = 20–30 mm; and very large = over 30 mm.

Common names of insects can also vary, and some insects found feeding on different plants may have the same common name. An example is the plume moth, a general term used for members of the family Pterophoridae. Plume moths exhibit a range of color patterns, and those with red-lined caterpillars are fairly common on plants of the sunflower family. It is difficult to know whether these represent a species complex or separate species, so I just refer to them all collectively as plume moths here. Some insects are generalists and occur on many different dune plants, while others are specialists and occur on only a single or several closely related plants. The generalists often occur in different locations and on different plant hosts every year, but the specialists are more predictable and can usually be found in the same habitat year after year, as long as their host plant remains.

This work is a tribute to the native strand and dune plants and their associated biota along the Pacific coast, many of which are near extinction as a result of human disturbance and displacement by invasive, nonindigenous flora. While exploring this sandy realm, remember the ancient Indian proverb: "Treat the earth well; it is not given to you by your parents, it was loaned to you by your children." Perhaps with greater understanding will come advocacy for the preservation of these unique habitats for your children and for future generations.

KELP COMMUNITY

In the shallow, sunlit offshore waters along the coast grow many species of marine algae, or wrack, the equivalent of terrestrial plant life. Like terrestrial plants, these seaweeds have chloroplasts and provide a food source for many marine creatures. These proliferate in communities analogous to our forests, meadows, and glens. The largest are seaweeds known as kelp. Species of kelp form a dense canopy at the ocean's surface.

In the understory of these forests are other seaweeds. These algae steadfastly hold on to the substrate to resist being torn loose by the ruthless surges of the waves as the tides and currents pull on them incessantly. When they finally lose their grip, many are brought by the tides and waves onto the strand.

An entire web of life depends on kelp and seaweed that is stranded on the beach, and it represents a self-contained community populated by a range of organisms adapted to feeding on it. These animals that feed on dead and decaying material are called detritivores. Detritivores are, in turn, food for a variety of predators and parasites from small mites to large birds. Microorganisms such as fungi, protozoa, and bacteria also play a role in the decomposition of kelp and seaweed. Can you imagine a beach without detritivores disposing of the kelp as it washes up day after day, week after week, for months and even years? In areas where the offshore kelp forests are extensive, it would take only a short time for the strand to become impassable.

The major consumers of kelp are beach hoppers, also known as sand fleas. These small crustaceans that congregate under piles of kelp are voracious eaters and are responsible for recycling about 50 percent of the deposited kelp. They can become quite numerous and at times the sand seems to be jumping with them. They are the favorite food of sandpipers, which pick them out of the sand when the tide is retreating during the day. At night many fall victim to pictured rove beetles that crush them in their mandibles and suck up their body liquids.

Kelp flies are the first insects to arrive, and the females waste no time looking for sites to deposit their eggs among the tangled debris. The pearly white eggs rapidly hatch, sometimes within as little as 24 hours, into maggots that quickly bore into the thick kelp stems to be protected before the next high tide or another group of scavengers arrives. The adult kelp flies use their lapping mouthparts to feed on practically everything from bird droppings to dead marine invertebrates, but their young feed exclusively on sea kelp.

Living on kelp is not without its dangers, because the fly larvae feeding in the wrack hardly ever go unnoticed. Beach rove beetles equipped with strong mandibles make short work of kelp flies. Marbled godwits and western willets feed on the larvae and puparia, and the emergence of the new adult flies attracts barn and violet-green swallows, which glide down to snap up as many as possible. Then there are the hawk flies that attack unwary kelp flies.

Bits and pieces of kelp left after the kelp flies have finished are food for other organisms, such as the little brown kelp weevil and kelp darkling beetle, whose larvae develop on decaying kelp. Other organisms prefer kelp in even later stages of decay. Marine springtails that look like small black dots often pepper the yellow stalks of decaying kelp stems. Springtails actually do have a spring under their abdomen that propels them rapidly through the air to land a few centimeters away from their original position.

Many marine mites are detritivores and feed on decaying kelp. Some possess robust and strongly curved claws to maintain their hold on the seaweed while their long, pointed mouthparts extract food particles. Other types of mites also share this habitat, including small red predaceous ones that patrol the kelp and surrounding sands looking for tiny organisms to eat.

One of the strangest animals I found crawling on the surface of a kelp stem was no more than a glob of protoplasm with a pair of eyes to tell me which was the front end. It was actually a minute free-living flatworm and had no problem moving around on the seaweed stalks.

KELP COMMUNITY		
Detritivores	Predators	Omnivores
Beach hopper	Western sandpiper	Striped shore crab
Smooth kelp fly	Pictured rove beetle	
Spotted kelp fly	Beach rove beetle	
Hairy kelp fly	Slender rove beetle	
Slender kelp fly	Marbled godwit	
Kelp weevil	Violet-green swallow	
Marine springtail	Kelp hawk fly	
Kelp darkling beetle	Flatworm	
Marine mite		
Sowbug		
Fungi		
Protozoa		
Bacteria		

BULL KELP (*Nereocystis luetkeana*: Laminariales: Laminariaceae, above) and **GIANT KELP** (*Macrocystis pyrifera*: Laminariales: Laminariaceae)

Characteristics: Bull kelp produces elongated stalks from a basal holdfast. Numerous leaf blades arise from terminal gas bladders used for buoyancy. Giant kelp also has basal stalks arising from a holdfast, but a single gas bladder occurs at the base of each blade.

Habitat and range: These species occur along the Pacific coast from Alaska to Baja California.

Comments: These two species of kelp produce "forests" that provide a habitat for one set of animals in the sea and another group when stranded on the beach.

BEACH HOPPER

(*Orchestoidea* sp.: Amphipoda: Talitridae)

Characteristics: Body midsized, smooth, curved, laterally flattened, with three pairs of feeding legs, five pairs of walking legs, and three pairs of modified jumping legs; small head with a single pair of large eyes and two unequal pairs of antennae.

Habitat and range: In burrows and under decaying seaweed and driftwood all along the Pacific coast in the high to middle intertidal zones.

Comments: These small crustaceans prefer decaying kelp but will also feed on other dead items along the beach. They are important food items for shorebirds.

WESTERN SANDPIPER
(Calidris mauri)

Characteristics: Small brown speckled shorebird with white stomach, long black bill, and black legs. There is a faint ear patch, and the head and upper breast may also be speckled. Coloration varies depending on maturity and season.

Habitat and range: Occurs along Pacific beaches from Washington to Baja California.

Comments: Beach hoppers are its favorite food.

PICTURED ROVE BEETLE
(Thinopinus pictus: Coleoptera: Staphylinidae)

Characteristics: Large, robust, flightless yellow beetle with dark markings on the dorsal surface and sickle-shaped toothed mandibles; larva similar to adult but lacks wing pads.

Habitat and range: On beaches along the Pacific coast from Alaska to Baja California.

Comments: Although they are well camouflaged, these beetles hide under kelp, driftwood, and other beach debris during the day and patrol the strand for prey, especially beach hoppers, at night.

STRIPED SHORE CRAB
(Pachygrapsus crassipes: Decapoda: Grapsidae)

Characteristics: Carapace square, purple to black, with transverse green stripes; claws red to purple; legs purple to black with flecks of green.

Habitat and range: Occurs in burrows and crevices and under rocks from Vancouver Island to Baja California.

Comments: This crab is semiterrestrial and will leave the water for hours to scour the beach for food. It feeds on algae and dead animals as well as intertidal invertebrates.

SMOOTH KELP FLY

(*Coelopa vanduzeei*: Diptera: Coelopidae)
Characteristics: Small, flattened gray fly with short, sparse hairs, small brownish eyes, gray head and thorax, and clear wings.
Habitat and range: On wrack along the Pacific coast from Washington to Mexico.
Comments: During the summer, when kelp accumulates on the beach, generation time is short and kelp flies can become quite numerous. The white larvae develop on decaying kelp and other seaweeds, but the adults will feed on animal matter as well.

SPOTTED KELP FLY

(*Helcomyza* sp.: Diptera: Helcomyzidae)
Characteristics: Midsized, flattened, grayish-brown fly with reddish-brown eyes, thorax with two longitudinal tan bands, and wings with black spots.
Habitat and range: The genus occurs on wrack along the Pacific coast from Washington to Mexico.
Comments: The white maggots feed on moist sea wrack.

HAIRY KELP FLY

(*Coelopa frigida*: Diptera: Coelopidae)
Characteristics: Large bristly fly with brown body, legs with dense patches of long hairs, head relatively small compared to body, and unspotted wings slightly tinted brown.
Habitat and range: All along the Pacific coast and elsewhere.
Comments: This is the most widely distributed seaweed fly known, occurring along ocean beaches in Europe and Asia as well as North America. The adults are slow moving and somewhat easy to capture. The smooth white larvae develop on decaying kelp and other seaweeds.

SLENDER KELP FLY

(*Fucellia maritima*: Diptera: Anthomyiidae)

Characteristics: Midsized slender fly with large, bare brown eyes, slender and bristly legs, and brownish wings.

Habitat and range: Associated with wrack from Washington to Mexico.

Comments: This is a representative of yet another family of kelp flies whose larvae develop on wrack stranded on the beach.

KELP FLY LARVA

(Diptera: Coelopidae)

Characteristics: Wormlike white maggot with head end pointed and posterior end truncate; head with a pair of black mouth hooks.

Habitat and range: Associated with decomposing kelp all along the Pacific coast from Alaska to Mexico.

Comments: It is difficult to separate the larvae of the various species of kelp flies without a microscope, since size and shape depend on age and nutrient availability. To avoid predators, the larvae enter the sand and feed on the underside of seaweed. If disturbed, they quickly dig into the sand to avoid capture.

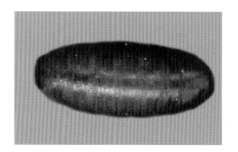

KELP FLY PUPARIUM

(Diptera: Coelopidae)

Characteristics: Hard, football-shaped case, light brown when first formed, becoming dark brown to black at maturity.

Habitat and range: Associated with decomposing kelp all along the Pacific coast from Alaska to Mexico.

Comments: Here is where the kelp fly maggot transforms into an adult kelp fly. The pupal period varies from several days to several weeks, depending on the temperature. The puparia are usually formed in the sand near the larval feeding sites. Shorebirds seek out puparia washed out of the sand by waves.

BEACH ROVE BEETLE

(*Hadrotes crassus*: Coleoptera: Staphylinidae)

Characteristics: Large, long, robust black beetle with a large, shiny head and pronotum, abbreviated elytra, dark legs, and tibia and tarsi with numerous spines.
Habitat and range: All along the Pacific coast from Washington to Baja California.
Comments: Kelp flies are a favorite food item.

SLENDER ROVE BEETLE

(*Pontomalota* sp.: Coleoptera: Staphylinidae)

Characteristics: Small, elongated, narrow black body with a small head; prothorax with rounded sides; wing pads short; bases of legs and antennae light brown to tan.
Habitat and range: Intertidal zone from Canada to Mexico along the Pacific coast.
Comments: Like many of the intertidal beetles, this species is flightless. It feeds on smaller insects, such as kelp weevils and darkling beetles, in the drier kelp deposits near the high tide line.

MARBLED GODWIT

(*Limosa fedoa*)

Characteristics: Large shorebird with long, dark legs, tan breast feathers, and back and tail feathers streaked with dark brown and white; bill long, pointed, orange at base, upturned slightly toward the tip.
Habitat and range: Shores and tide flats from Alaska to Mexico during the winter and early spring.
Comments: This is one of several shorebirds that leave the water's edge to feed on kelp fly larvae and puparia in the intertidal zone. These insects provide a change from their normal diet of intertidal invertebrates.

VIOLET-GREEN SWALLOW
(*Tachycineta thalassina*)
Characteristics: Back greenish-black, head and wings dark purplish, underparts white, eye partially encircled by a white band.
Habitat and range: Breeds in various settings all along the Pacific coast during the summer. Winters farther south.
Comments: They swoop back and forth over piles of decaying kelp or patches of marram grass to catch various insects on the wing.

KELP HAWK FLY
(*Aphrostylus direptor.* Diptera: Empididae)
Characteristics: Midsized brown body with a metallic sheen; projecting head with large eyes, attached near base of swollen thorax; antennae with apical bristle; wings darkly tinted.
Habitat and range: Wrack on shores from Washington to California.
Comments: This predator searches for kelp flies and other small invertebrates in the intertidal zone.

KELP WEEVIL
(*Emphyastes fucicola*: Coleoptera: Curculionidae)
Characteristics: Small, tan to brown adult with short snout and reduced antennae; body curved ventrally, smooth; larvae white with tan head, C-shaped, curved ventrally, with reduced legs.
Habitat and range: Drying wrack in upper intertidal zone from Oregon to Baja California.
Comments: Kelp weevils seek out wrack that has partially dried but is still moist. The adults fold their legs against their body and remain motionless when disturbed. The larvae feed while in contact with damp sand under drying seaweed.

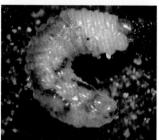

MARINE SPRINGTAIL

(*Anurida maritima*: Collembola: Neanuridae)

Characteristics: Small, elongated, cylindrical grayish body with clearly visible segments and short antennae; terminus of abdomen with furca or jumping organ.

Habitat and range: Lower intertidal zone all along the Pacific coast.

Comments: Marine springtails will feed on both animal and plant matter. They are very abundant and are considered to be important scavengers along the seashore. Their coating of hydrophobic hairs makes it impossible to hold them underwater or even to wet their bodies. Their aggregations are an example of homotypic agglutination.

KELP DARKLING BEETLE

(*Epantius obscurus*: Coleoptera: Tenebrionidae)

Characteristics: Midsized dark brown beetle with a small head that can be withdrawn under the edge of the pronotum, which has rounded sides; eyes small, slightly protruding from sides of head; antennae bead-like; elytra with longitudinal striations.

Habitat and range: High intertidal zone from Oregon to Baja California.

Comments: The adults are slow moving but difficult to locate.

MARINE MITE

(Trombidiformes: Halacaridae)

Characteristics: Features vary depending on the type of marine mite; adult minute, with eight legs, simple palpi with narrow outstretched tips, and strongly curved claws on all legs.

Habitat and range: In kelp and under rocks, driftwood, and other debris all along the Pacific coast.

Comments: This is one of many marine mites of the family Halacaridae that feed on seaweed in the intertidal zone.

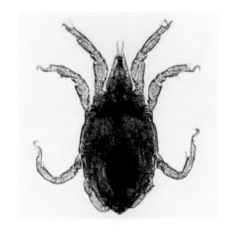

SOWBUG
(*Alloniscus* sp.: Isopoda: Alloniscidae)
Characteristics: Small to large, slender, terrestrial crustacean covered with dark dorsal plates with edges curved backward; head horizontal, bearing two eyes and a pair of prominent antennae; seven pairs of legs and paired appendages (uropods) at the end of the abdomen.
Habitat and range: Along the Pacific coast from Canada to California.
Comments: The immature stages look like miniature adults. Since they respire with gills, they seek out areas of high humidity. They serve as food for shore-birds and carnivorous beetles.

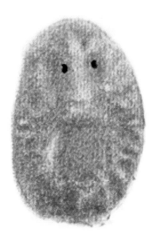

FREE-LIVING FLATWORM
(Platyhelminthes: Polycladida)
Characteristics: Small primitive inverte-brates with a flattened, oval, ciliated body surface and two dark eyes.
Habitat and range: These are associated with marine waters worldwide.
Comments: These simple animals live in wet sand or on stranded seaweed. They move slowly over the substrate and can bend their bodies into various shapes.

DRIFTWOOD COMMUNITY

Aside from kelp deposits, the shore is often littered with an assortment of drift-wood washed in on the tides. Some may have drifted on the tides for years before ending up on a beach some distance from its source. Once it has been beached far enough up on the strand, driftwood becomes the home of an assortment of creatures ranging from minute microbes to large beetles that use it for shelter and/or food. There are millipedes that curl up when disturbed, sowbugs that become immobile against the damp sand, small white worms that partly embed them-selves in the decaying wood, and spiders that look for prey. There may be beach hoppers that immediately jump away or bury themselves in the sand.

A variety of carnivorous ground beetles use wood just for shelter. Even though they remain hidden during the day and emerge only at night to feed, some have quite striking color patterns of black and brown hues. They also vary greatly in shape and have a hard exoskeleton that protects them from prey and from other predators.

In addition to those seeking shelter under driftwood, many insects feed on driftwood. Pulling apart rotting pieces of driftwood often exposes the most ef-ficient of these detritivores, termites. Their wood-eating activities are made pos-sible by protozoa in their guts. These protozoa, along with their own bacterial symbionts, digest wood particles for the termites. This amazing case of symbiosis evolved millions of years ago and shows how two groups of organisms have come to depend on each other to survive. In the spring, hordes of winged adults swarm out of their shelter to mate. Watchful birds know when the insects have started these courtship flights, and swallows and gulls grasp them in midair, while crows pick up those that are still on the ground. Later, many can be found on the beach with their wings broken off.

Aside from termites, some beetles also assist in the breakdown of wood. One wintry day, I noticed a crow chipping away at a half-exposed log protruding from a sand dune. Watching birds can be very helpful in locating insects. The crows had found a colony of large stag beetles and were intent on locating the fat, juicy larvae.

The larvae of many other beetles also develop in dead wood, and many take a long time to mature, thus becoming quite large in the meantime. Two additional beetles with wood-feeding larvae are the beach lucanid and the false blister beetle. However, the true giants of the strand are three longhorn beetles: the California prionus, pine sawyer, and banded alder borer. Their white larvae can take up to two to three years to mature and transform into adults.

One particular beetle that I am especially fond of is the minute driftwood weevil. This weevil spends its entire lifetime eating its way through decomposing wood. Living in such a gloomy place has reduced the size of its eyes, since they are probably not that useful anyway. Where this little weevil originally came from is a mystery, but it seems destined to spend the rest of its existence along the Pacific coast strand, since it occurs nowhere else in the world.

Breaking down driftwood is a continuous task, with new wood arriving all the time. The decomposition process involves a complex of microbes as well as the insects and millipedes discussed above. Many types of fungi assist in wood decay, and some show their presence by producing mushrooms, conks, and other fruiting bodies on the surface of the wood. Finally, disintegration of the oldest wood returns nutrients to the earth, thus providing nourishment for the strand plants.

Aside from the organisms associated with decomposing driftwood, the strand is home to a number of general predators. The semipalmated plover is a perfect example of the opportunistic feeders found among shorebirds that overwinter along the coast and migrate north to breed. This bird hunts close to the water, where it dines on small crustaceans, insects, mollusks, isopods, and marine worms. It has a peculiar method of trembling its foot in the sand in order to reveal the presence of these invertebrates. However, in summer its diet changes to predominantly insects hiding in the driftwood.

A closer look will reveal a multitude of insect predators, such as the gazelle fly. At first glance, the long, dark, hairy legs and absence of wings might make you think it's a spider, but it has only six legs. The eyes on this modified fly take up most of its head. While the gazelle fly does not fly, it can scurry over the sand at amazing speeds to catch its dinner. Then there are dance flies, with their long, daggerlike beak that can quickly dispatch smaller insects.

DRIFTWOOD COMMUNITY	
Detritivores	Predators/Omnivores
Millipedes	Ground beetles
White worms	Western tiger beetle
Termites	Western gull
Rugose stag beetle	American crow
Beach lucanid beetle	Semipalmated plover
False blister beetle	Gazelle fly
California prionus beetle	Dance fly
Pine sawyer beetle	Shore bug
Banded alder borer	Soft-winged flower beetle
Driftwood weevil	Dune crab spider
Red-belted conk fungus	Jumping spider
	Dune wolf spider
	Nematodes
	Protozoa
	Western yellow jacket

Another fascinating intertidal predatory insect often found under driftwood is the shore bug, which can survive submergence in seawater during high tides. These predators spend most of the day prowling around in the sand near the high tide mark looking for small life forms such as springtails to devour. But shore bugs themselves are victimized by a parasitic nematode that takes so much of their nutrients that the bugs are sterilized. Round, dark spheres of a protozoan parasite can also occur inside shore bugs. Sometimes life isn't fair, yet the shore bugs continue to survive.

Everything has one or more special features that allow it to survive in a hostile world. Some use camouflage, others concealment; a few taste bad while others masquerade as their distasteful comrades; and still others have chemical weapons. An example of a chemical defense mechanism is found in the soft-winged flower beetle, which occurs under driftwood and wrack. When danger threatens, two large vesicles that extrude from both sides of its body expel offensive chemicals onto potential predators. These chemicals have been characterized as batracho-toxins, which are highly potent cardio- and neurotoxic alkaloids. They are the same type of toxin that poison dart frogs and some birds use for protection.

The driftwood community has a number of spiders that are constantly on the alert for prey, whether it be insects or crustaceans. Little flattened dune crab spiders rest on the sand under pieces of driftwood, while bristly jumping spiders sit on the driftwood waiting for flies. On the sand prowling around stranded driftwood are fast-running, long-legged wolf spiders whose color patterns provide excellent camouflage against the background of beach sand. Wherever you look among the driftwood, it isn't difficult to find a spider.

DRIFTWOOD is wood carried up onto a beach by wind and waves. Some remains in the intertidal zone while the rest is washed up to the high tide line. The variety of driftwood on a beach is usually a reflection of the types of trees growing along adjacent rivers flowing into the ocean. Driftwood can originate from territories some distance away and even from across the Pacific Ocean. Organisms of the strand quickly establish themselves in and around this new resource. The condition of driftwood on the beach at any one time depends on the type of wood, how long it has been in the sea, and also on land and air temperature.

COAST MILLIPEDE

(*Bollmaniulus* sp.: Julida: Parajulidae)

Characteristics: Large to very large, long, shiny, brown-banded invertebrate with one pair of small eyes, a single pair of short antennae, and many body segments, each with two pairs of walking legs.

Habitat and range: Along the Pacific coast from Canada to California.

Comments: When disturbed, coast millipedes will coil and remain motionless.

WHITE WORM

(*Enchytraeus* sp.: Haplotaxida: Megascolecidae)

Characteristics: Small, soft, white annelid with numerous body segments, each one bearing a few short bristles; partially digested wood particles usually occur in the long intestine.

Habitat and range: Widespread throughout North America.

Comments: White worms will feed on a variety of decaying plant material including driftwood. They are hermaphroditic; each individual has both male and female reproductive organs. At times they exhibit homotypic agglutination.

BLACK-HEADED GROUND BEETLE

(*Bembidion transversale*: Coleoptera: Carabidae)

Characteristics: Small, shiny beetle with a black head and pronotum and brown wing covers (elytra); antennae brown, as long as head and prothorax combined; legs brown, long.

Habitat and range: Along the coast from Alaska to California.

Comments: These fast-running beetles rest under driftwood during the day and emerge at night to seek food.

ROUND GROUND BEETLE

(*Omophron ovale*: Coleoptera: Carabidae)

Characteristics: A small, smooth, oval beetle with a dorsal pattern of dark brown markings on a light brown background. The head is tightly appressed against the prothorax.

Habitat and range: Along the coast from Alaska to California.

Comments: This is an unusual shape for a ground beetle.

WAISTED GROUND BEETLE

(*Dyschirus obesus*: Coleoptera: Carabidae)

Characteristics: Small, completely tan beetle with a dark smudge in the center of the elytra; body constricted in the middle between the thorax and abdomen.

Habitat and range: Along the coast from Alaska to California.

Comments: The constricted waist and expanded prothorax quickly identify this beetle.

BLACK GROUND BEETLE

(*Pterostichus* sp.: Coleoptera: Carabidae)

Characteristics: Midsized black beetle with the sides of the pronotum ridged and the elytra with distinct longitudinal lines (striae).

Habitat and range: Along the coast from Alaska to California.

Comments: These beetles will emerge on cloudy days as well as at night to seek food.

WESTERN TIGER BEETLE

(*Cicindela oregona*: Coleoptera: Carabidae)

Characteristics: Midsized, metallic green to gray beetle with white markings on the elytra and long, bristly, slender legs.

Habitat and range: Along the coast from Alaska to California.

Comments: Since these beetles hunt by sight, they are active during the day, running and flying after prey and searching for mates.

SUBTERRANEAN TERMITE

(*Reticulitermes hesperus*: Isoptera: Rhinotermitidae)

Characteristics: Small, soft-bodied, yellowish workers with large heads and beaded antennae; adults dark brown to black, with long, fuscous, membranous wings.

Habitat and range: Found throughout western North America.

Comments: These social insects have three basic castes; workers, soldiers, and reproductives (adults). They are the most important wood-destroying insects in North America. Those found in driftwood usually form small colonies. Bacteria and protozoa in their gut assist in digesting the wood.

DAMPWOOD TERMITE

(*Zootermopsis nevadensis*: Isoptera: Archotermopsidae)

Characteristics: Midsized, soft-bodied, yellowish workers with large heads and beaded antennae; adults similar in color to workers, with long, clear, membranous wings.

Habitat and range: Found throughout western North America.

Comments: Dampwood termites prefer decaying driftwood partially covered with sand, thus maintaining a high degree of moisture. Colonies can get quite large and the winged adults often emerge in masses in late spring or summer.

DRIFTWOOD COMMUNITY

TERMITE PROTOZOAN

(*Trichonympha* sp.: Trichomonadida: Trichonymphidae)

Characteristics: With a cone-like base and hemispheric cap, these protozoa resemble ice cream cones. They bear cilia that make them quite mobile.

Habitat and range: In the gut of dampwood termites.

Comments: These protozoa do not produce cellulase but contain endosymbiotic bacteria that produce cellulase to digest wood. Similar protozoans have been found in 100-million-year-old termite remains.

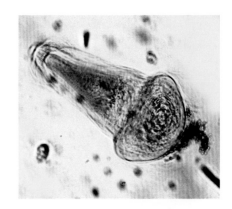

WESTERN GULL

(*Larus occidentalis*)

Characteristics: A large gull with black wings and back, white head and breast, pinkish feet, and a slightly hooked yellow beak with a red spot on the tip of the lower bill.

Habitat and range: Western gulls are yearlong residents along the entire Pacific coast.

Comments: Western gulls will eat insects on the wing as well as those among driftwood and kelp. They are very bold and like to construct their nests on rooftops. Wooden owls positioned on roofs to frighten the gulls are often ignored.

AMERICAN CROW

(*Corvus brachyrhynchos*)

Characteristics: A large, stout, completely black bird with a strong, pointed beak; sexes similar in appearance.

Habitat and range: A yearlong resident along the entire Pacific coast.

Comments: These crows constantly scour the beaches for various food items including insects associated with driftwood.

RUGOSE STAG BEETLE

(*Sinodendron rugosum*: Coleoptera: Lucanidae)

Characteristics: Midsized, black to dark brown beetle with clubbed antennae; dorsal surface covered with small pits, producing a rugose appearance.

Habitat and range: Adults occur under driftwood along the Pacific Northwest coast.

Comments: The adults are very slow moving and easily captured.

RUGOSE STAG BEETLE LARVA

(*Sinodendron rugosum*: Coleoptera: Lucanidae)

Characteristics: Midsized, C-shaped white grub with a brown head capsule and six short legs.

Habitat and range: In decaying driftwood along the Pacific Northwest coast.

Comments: These larvae feed on the wood, but like termites, they cannot digest it. Their hindgut is composed of a large fermentation chamber where the wood is digested by microorganisms. Among these organisms are pinworms that multiply without causing the beetle any ill effects.

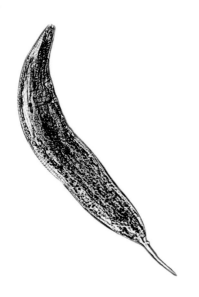

PINWORM

(Nematoda: Thelastomatidae)

Characteristics: Microscopic worm (nematode) with a thick body lacking segments; a narrow, blunt head; and a pointed tail.

Habitat and range: Live in the gut of rugose stag beetle grubs and adults along the Pacific Northwest coast.

Comments: These nematodes feed on bacteria and other microorganisms and are not pathogenic. Eggs pass out with the feces and are ingested by other grubs.

BEACH LUCANID BEETLE
(*Platyceropsis keeni*: Coleoptera: Lucanidae)

Characteristics: Midsized, shiny, metallic dark beetle with clubbed antennae and bristly legs; pronotum almost as wide as elytra.

Habitat and range: Larvae develop in decaying driftwood and adults occur on beach vegetation and under driftwood along the Pacific coast from Alaska to California.

Comments: Adults bury themselves in the sand when disturbed.

FALSE BLISTER BEETLE
(*Ditylus quadricollis*: Coleoptera: Oedemeridae)

Characteristics: Large, dark brown to black beetle with long, nonclubbed antennae, protruding eyes, and a pronotum narrower than the elytra. The body is covered with a dense layer of short hairs.

Habitat and range: Associated with driftwood along the Pacific coast from Washington to California.

Comments: The larvae develop in driftwood.

CALIFORNIA PRIONUS BEETLE
(*Prionus californicus*: Coleoptera: Cerambycidae)

Characteristics: Very large (up to 55 mm long), broad, smooth, dark brown (elytra often tinged reddish) beetle with long, thick, saw-toothed antennae and robust legs. The sides of the pronotum have three large projecting spines.

Habitat and range: Associated with various types of wood throughout the Pacific Northwest.

Comments: This is the second largest of the coastal beetles. It takes the wood-eating larva several years to complete its development.

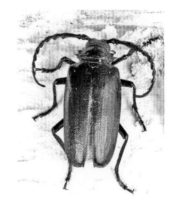

PINE SAWYER BEETLE

(*Ergates spiculatus*: Coleoptera:
Cerambycidae)

Characteristics: Very large (up to 68
mm in length), chestnut-brown, smooth,
elliptical beetle with long but narrow
antennae and slender legs. The sides of the
pronotum bear many small spines. Larvae
white, also very large, with distinct body
segments and brown spiracles.
Habitat and range: Throughout the
Pacific Northwest in association with
various types of wood.
Comments: This is the largest coastal
beetle, and the adults are hard to miss
when they are resting on logs. Crows and
gulls tear open decaying driftwood logs
searching for the wood-eating larvae.

BANDED ALDER BORER

(*Rosalia funebris*: Coleoptera:
Cerambycidae)

Characteristics: Very large, slender beetle
with white bands across the black elytra
and a black diamond in the middle of the
gray pronotum; antennae longer than the
body, with alternating black and white
patches.
Habitat and range: Larvae develop on
a variety of hardwoods throughout the
Pacific Northwest.
Comments: The banded alder borer is
well camouflaged when it rests on weath-
ered driftwood after its spring emergence.

DRIFTWOOD WEEVIL

(*Elassoptes marinus*: Coleoptera:
Curculionidae)

Characteristics: Small, shiny, dark brown
to reddish-brown weevil with small eyes,
short antennae, and a short, stout beak.
Legs short, all bearing a long spine at the
tip.
Habitat and range: Found in driftwood
along the Pacific Northwest coast.
Comments: These weevils often feed
together in tunnels they make in driftwood. Since they rarely leave the tunnels,
their eyes are reduced.

RED-BELTED CONK FUNGUS

(*Fomitopsis pinicola*: Polyporales: Fomitopsidaceae)

Characteristics: Fruiting body attached laterally to wood surface; flesh hard, tough; top white gray, whitish along margin; pores on underside small, white to pale yellow.

Habitat and range: Grows on dead trees, usually conifer logs, washed up on the beach; cosmopolitan.

Comments: This fungus is a major destroyer of conifer logs washed up on the coast. Small, elongated fly larvae (Diptera: Chironomidae) feed on the underside of the conk and chew small excavations into the pores.

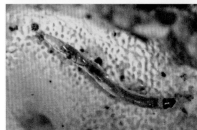

SEMIPALMATED PLOVER

(*Charadrius semipalmatus*)

Characteristics: Small, plump, brown-backed bird with a single dark breast band, short yellow bill that is black at the tip, and orange legs.

Habitat and range: Coastal strands and dunes in the Pacific Northwest from fall to spring.

Comments: This species is well camouflaged against a background of driftwood. It harbors a variety of commensal and parasitic organisms, including feather lice, feather mites, tapeworms, roundworms, and flukes. The latter three groups of internal parasites are acquired from eating crustaceans that carry the infective stages.

GAZELLE FLY

(*Chersodromia* sp.: Diptera: Hybotidae)

Characteristics: Small, dark, flightless fly with huge bare eyes; short, two-segmented antennae; and long, bristly legs.

Habitat and range: Along the Pacific coast from Washington to California.

Comments: The gazelle fly runs and hops quite rapidly over rocks in pursuit of prey.

DANCE FLY

(*Rhamphomyia* sp.: Diptera: Empididae)
Characteristics: Midsized fly with large, bare eyes; antennae positioned in the middle of the head; a long, narrow proboscis; and clear wings with gray on the outer edges.
Habitat and range: Coastal strand from Alaska to California.
Comments: The proboscis is quite long in proportion to the head.

SHORE BUG

(*Saldula laticollis*: Hemiptera: Saldidae)
Characteristics: Small, dark-colored bug with protruding eyes, medium-sized antennae, well-developed, bristly legs, and wing covers with white spots.
Habitat and range: Along the Pacific coast from Canada to California.
Comments: Shore bugs fly in short spurts but usually chase down their prey. They often occur under the leaves of strand plants where they encounter their enemy, the dune dwarf spider. Shore bugs can survive immersion in seawater for short periods and are parasitized by a nematode and a protozoan (see the following).

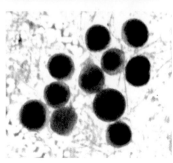

SHORE BUG NEMATODE PARASITE

(*Halophilanema prolata*: Tylenchida: Allantonematidae)
Characteristics: Microscopic, slender worm lacking segments; parasitic females elongated and tubular, containing eggs and juveniles.
Habitat and range: Thus far, found only in shore bugs on the strand in Oregon.
Comments: Infected bugs have reduced fat body and reproductive organs.

SHORE BUG PROTOZOAN PARASITE

(Protozoa: Eugregarinorida)
Characteristics: Microscopic cysts in the body cavity of shore bugs appear as round, dark balls. Each cyst contains spores that can infect healthy shore bugs.
Habitat and range: Found only in shore bugs on the strand in Oregon.
Comments: Infected bugs have reduced fat body.

SOFT-WINGED FLOWER BEETLE

(*Endeodes collaris*: Coleoptera: Melyridae)
Characteristics: Small, elongated beetle, black except for the red pronotum, with bead-like antennae, protruding black head, and slender legs.
Habitat and range: High intertidal zone from Washington to California.
Comments: When threatened, these beetles can release toxic chemicals from gland openings on the sides of their bodies.

DUNE CRAB SPIDER

(*Xysticus* sp.: Araneae: Thomisidae)
Characteristics: Small, somewhat flattened spider with the carapace (anterior body part) having a central light band extending back from the eyes. Legs held in crab-like fashion.
Habitat and range: On ground under driftwood all along the Pacific coast.
Comments: These spiders are ambush hunters and do not build webs.

JUMPING SPIDER

(*Phidippus* sp.: Araneae: Salticidae)
Characteristics: Small, bristly black spider with rows of white spots on the abdomen, forward-facing eyes, and legs with white bands.
Habitat and range: On ground, including under driftwood all along the Pacific coast.
Comments: These spiders depend on their excellent vision to catch prey. Silk is used only to protect the eggs and provide a "lifeline" in an emergency.

DUNE WOLF SPIDER

(*Arctosa* sp.: Araneae: Lycosidae)

Characteristics: Large, light-colored spider with two longitudinal brown bars on the carapace, white spots on the abdomen, and striped legs bearing three tarsal claws.

Habitat and range: Coastal dunes and strand areas from Alaska to Mexico.

Comments: These spiders are well camouflaged against the sandy background. The female attaches the egg sac to her spinnerets and the hatchlings are carried on their mother's back until they can survive on their own.

WESTERN YELLOW JACKET

(*Vespula pensylvanica*: Hymenoptera: Vespidae)

Characteristics: Small (worker) or large (queen) black and yellow wasps with a diamond-shaped black mark on the first abdominal segment and a complete yellow ring surrounding the eye.

Habitat and range: Along the Pacific coast from Washington to California and elsewhere.

Comments: The workers are often encountered during the late spring or summer among dried driftwood in the foredunes. They alight on selected pieces and scrape fibers from the surface. They use the fibers in constructing or enlarging the nest, which can be above or below ground. The workers are quite bold and will not hesitate to sting if molested. They prey on a range of invertebrates and scavenge dead protein sources, including picnic items.

STRAND PLANT COMMUNITIES

The strand, whose borders are defined by the lowest reaches of a minus tide and the surge of the highest full tide, is a harsh environment. Plants living there not only have to survive an intermittent dosing of seawater but are assailed by offshore winds that test the strength of their stems, leaves, and roots, grind abrasive sand particles against them, and occasionally bury them entirely. It is no wonder that strand plants are small and have deep taproots, fleshy leaves, and protective hairs or other devices to lessen the caustic effects of the blowing sand and restless surf.

The majority of strand plants are annuals that disappear during the winter gales. Some survive the first year and manage to flower the following year. A very few with long taproots may survive for several years and can be called short-lived perennials. Of utmost importance to the survival and distribution of strand plants is having waterproof seedpods that withstand abrasion by sand, pounding by breakers, and often floating for months in the currents. Strand plants are found from the middle of the strand zone to the top of the high tide level. In this region, they have little competition from other vegetation, especially the thick mats of beach grass that have spread throughout the sand dunes.

SEA ROCKET

Sea rocket is one of the most common plants of the strand and is as seafaring as any naval vessel, which is why you can find it growing on most beaches in the world. Its floating seedpods, each of which contains a single seed so tightly attached to the corky fruit that it is impossible to remove, can withstand months of floating in the sea. There are two species along the Pacific coast. European sea rocket, with toothed leaves, originally came from Europe, and American sea rocket, with nearly entire leaves, came from the Eastern Seaboard and reached the Pacific coast in the 1880s.

The succulent tissues of sea rocket are similar to those of desert plants. While there is no lack of water on the beach, it is all salty and unusable until plants can convert it to freshwater. Sea rocket does that by storing the removed salt in its tissues; if you select these leaves for salad, you will need no salt in the dressing.

Bumblebees, cabbage butterflies, alfalfa butterflies, painted lady butterflies, and hoverflies feed on nectar in sea rocket flower spikes. Some butterflies leave a few eggs on the plants before they depart, and in spite of the salty tissue, the caterpillars manage to complete their development. Little green cabbage aphids also seek out these plants. Since summer populations are hermaphroditic and reproduce continuously, these aphids can form dense clusters on sea rocket.

Other insects have adapted to sea rocket. Dark wavy lines on the leaves indicate that leaf-mining maggots are using sea rocket as one of their host plants. You can see the twisty path of the maggot become wider from where it hatched to its final pupal chamber. Developing within the leaf provides not only an ample supply of food, but also protection from salt, wind, and rain.

The European diamondback moth is a cabbage pest, and it didn't take long for it to find sea rocket in its Pacific setting. The small green caterpillars first make a safety net around themselves to keep from being blown off the plant before they can consume the developing flower heads and seedpods. Unfortunately, the webbing is too flimsy to protect them from enemies, and parasitic wasps inject their own eggs into the caterpillars.

Even the roots of sea rocket don't escape notice. Several types of caterpillars live in the sand around the roots of strand and dune plants. They are brown, just like the sand, and some have a spattering of fine dots that resemble sand particles on their backs.

Little shore flies rest on the leaves of sea rocket. The large mouths of these flies are often open, giving the impression that they are laughing. They use their mouthparts to scrape food from the surface of the plants.

Tiny eight-legged spider mites also test the juices of sea rocket. These minute mites cause havoc with many cultivated crops. Since they are wingless, how did they reach these isolated plants? Their elongated front legs, typical of those of many spider mites, are held out like antennae to test the surroundings.

Late in the season, large black spots caused by a fungus occur on the plants, especially on the developing seedpods. The growing fungus makes an almost perfect circle on the plant tissue. Snails don't seem to mind eating fungus-infected seedpods along with normal ones.

SEA ROCKET COMMUNITY	
Herbivores	Parasites
Orange sulfur butterfly	Fungal blight
American painted lady butterfly	Diamondback moth wasp
Cabbage aphid	
Leaf-mining fly	
Diamondback moth	
Sand caterpillar	
Shore fly	
Spider mite	

AMERICAN SEA ROCKET (*Cakile edentula*) and **EUROPEAN SEA ROCKET** (*C. maritima*: Brassicaceae)

Characteristics: Fleshy, upright to spreading stems; leaves entire to lobed (*C. edentula*) or deeply toothed or dissected (*C. maritima*); purplish-pink to white flowers from May to November; seedpods (fruits) large, fleshy, two-jointed, with lower joint smooth (*C. edentula*) or with a pair of triangular protuberances (*C. maritima*); seeds embedded in pods.

Habitat and range: Coastal strands from Alaska to Baja California.

Comments: Aside from those listed below, the following insects also visit the flowers and may serve as pollinators: woodland skipper (*Ochlodes sylvanoides*), purplish copper butterfly (*Epidemia helloides*), bumblebees (*Bombus* spp.) and flower flies (*Eristalis* spp.).

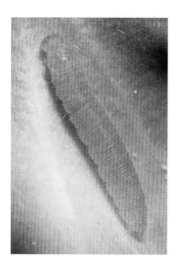

ORANGE SULFUR BUTTERFLY CATERPILLAR

(*Colias eurytheme*: Lepidoptera: Pieridae)

Characteristics: Small, slender green caterpillar covered with short, erect hairs. Adult butterfly yellow with black outer wing borders.

Habitat and range: I found this species only on American sea rocket in Oregon.

Comments: The orange sulfur butterfly has a wide host range, and sea rocket is probably only an occasional host plant.

AMERICAN PAINTED LADY BUTTERFLY

(*Vanessa virginiensis*: Lepidoptera: Nymphalidae)

Characteristics: Very large butterfly; wings mostly orange with black, brown, and white markings; hind wings with two black-bordered blue spots along the outer margins.

Habitat and range: Throughout North America.

Comments: This is a common butterfly that visits many different flowers besides those of sea rocket. The larvae can develop on a range of plants but seem to prefer those of the mustard family.

CABBAGE APHID

(*Lipaphis pseudobrassicae*: Hemiptera: Aphididae)

Characteristics: A small, plump, greenish aphid with short antennae and dark eyes. The reproductive stages are wingless.

Habitat and range: Throughout the Pacific coast and elsewhere.

Comments: This is a cosmopolitan species that prefers plants of the mustard family. Cabbage aphids suck plant juices from stems and leaves of sea rocket. Populations can build up significantly during the warm summer months. Parasitic wasps deposit eggs inside the aphids' bodies.

LEAF-MINING FLY

(*Liriomyza* sp.: Diptera: Agromyzidae)

Characteristics: Larvae are small, elongated, and pale, with dark mouth hooks. They develop within the leaf mines. Adult flies are small and brownish on the back, with large reddish eyes, clear wings, and long legs.

Habitat and range: Sea rocket in Oregon.

Comments: The mines are irregular and usually do not cover the entire leaf. These flies are uncommon and appear to prefer American rather than European sea rocket.

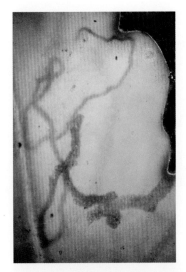

DIAMONDBACK MOTH

(*Plutella xylostella*: Lepidoptera: Plutellidae)

Characteristics: Caterpillar small, greenish, with brown head; pupa with brown and white stripes, formed in an open, netlike silk cocoon at the base of the plant. Adult moth small, brown, slender, with a row of lighter scales arranged in the shape of diamonds running down the back when at rest.

Habitat and range: Widespread throughout the western states.

Comments: The larvae bind flower parts together with silk while feeding and are parasitized by wasps (Hymenoptera: Braconidae) that form their cocoons within those of the diamondback moth (lower right).

SAND CATERPILLAR

(*Lasionycta* sp.: Lepidoptera: Noctuidae)

Characteristics: Large, sand-colored caterpillar, often with darker horizontal stripes and spots on the body.

Habitat and range: Sand caterpillars occur along the entire Pacific coast.

Comments: This is one of several species of sand caterpillar that feed on a range of strand and dune plants. Beware when handling them since their mandibles can deliver a painful bite. They can quickly bury themselves in the sand.

SHORE FLY
(Diptera: Ephydridae)

Characteristics: Small brownish fly with a large head and eyes, small antennae, and spotted wings.

Habitat and range: Strands and dunes along the Pacific Northwest coast.

Comments: The huge mouth is used for scraping algae and bacteria off various substrates. Shore fly maggots can tolerate high salt levels in their habitats.

SPIDER MITE
(Bryobiinae: Tetranychidae)

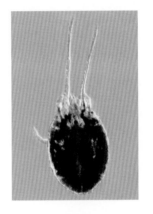

Characteristics: Small brownish mite with the front pair of legs much longer than the other three pairs.

Habitat and range: I found this species only on American sea rocket in Oregon.

Comments: Many spider mites produce webbing, but I found no silk associated with these sea rocket mites.

FUNGAL BLIGHT
(*Ascochyta* sp.: Ascomycota: Pleosporales)

Characteristics: Large, round, blister-like black spots surrounded by minute fungal bodies (pycnidia) immersed in sea rocket. The spores (conidia) are ovoid to oblong and two-celled.

Habitat and range: Strands from Washington to California.

Comments: The round black areas of necrosis are most conspicuous on the seedpods.

SEA SANDWORT

Sea sandwort is the most pristine of all the strand plants. Its small, succulent green leaves are so smooth that sand grains can't adhere to them. Thus the leaves as well as the small flowers with their five tiny white petals always appear immaculate. Dense clusters of stems provide protection for the large, black lucanid beetles found along the strand that spend their time nibbling on the leaves and searching for mates.

The leaf color of sea sandwort is very consistent, which makes it easy to detect the activities of fly maggots that feed on the internal tissues and cause the leaves to turn grayish brown. Healthy maggots consume leaf after leaf, working their way down the stem and forming a puparium inside the final leaf. Although the leaf-mining maggots are well hidden, some fall victim to a bacterial infection and never have a chance to form a puparium.

In the sand around the roots of sea sandwort and other plants can be found the elongated larvae, short pupae, and oval brown adults of the ciliated sand beetle. The slender, tubelike larvae glide through the sand grains consuming roots while the adults patrol the surrounding surface for mates and food during the day. Living under sand does not protect a beetle larva from attacks by a parasitic fly that deposits her eggs on the larva's head. When the fly maggots hatch, they burrow into and consume the beetle larva, destroying the insect before it can finish its development.

The presence of nocturnal insect activity can be detected the following morning by tracks made during the night by ciliated sand beetles. These tracks consist of a solid line where the body rubs against the sand, and dimples on each side of the line that represent leg imprints. These minute trails can extend for yards over the sand, skirting around driftwood or plants and then suddenly disappearing, as if their makers were suddenly lifted up into the sky. The tracks soon vanish as the morning breeze covers the imprints with sand.

SEA SANDWORT COMMUNITY		
Herbivores	Parasites	Symbionts
Stag beetle	Tachinid fly	Phoretic nematodes
Leaf-mining fly	Bacterial disease	
Ciliated sand beetle		

SEA SANDWORT
(*Honckenya peploides*: Caryophyllaceae)
Characteristics: Succulent herb with
upright to prostrate stems; leaves fleshy,
opposite, pointed at tip; flowers white
or greenish, on short stalks in leaf axils;
petals five, separate, equal in size to sepals;
stamens eight to ten; fruits spherical
leathery capsules longer than sepals;
flowers from May to September.
Habitat and range: Coastal strands,
dunes, tidal marshes from Alaska to
southern Oregon; also along North
American Atlantic coast and in Eurasia.
Comments: This plant is very resistant to
attacks by insects and plant pathogens.

STAG BEETLE
(*Platyceroides agassii*: Coleoptera:
Lucanidae)
Characteristics: Midsized, shiny,
flightless black beetle with short, clubbed
antennae and reddish legs.
Habitat and range: Strands and dunes
along the Pacific coast.
Comments: The white larvae develop in
driftwood and the adults nibble the leaves
of sea sandwort and carry nematodes
(Diplogastridae) under their wing covers.

LEAF-MINING FLY

(*Delia* sp.: Diptera: Anthomyiidae)

Characteristics: Maggots small, white; pupae tan to dark brown depending on maturity. Adults small, gray, with large brown eyes, clear wings, and dark longitudinal lines on the thorax.

Habitat and range: Strands and dunes in Washington and Oregon.

Comments: The maggots consume the soft, moist inner leaf tissues, eating their way down the plant until they are ready to pupate. Some killed by a bacterial infection become reddish.

STRAND PLANT COMMUNITIES: SEA SANDWORT

CILIATED SAND BEETLE

(*Coelus ciliatus*: Coleoptera:
Tenebrionidae)

Characteristics: Larvae small, elongated,
wormlike, yellow, with a tan head and
thorax. Pupae small, yellowish brown,
slightly curved, formed free in the sand.
Adults small, oval, shiny, dark brown.

Habitat and range: Along the coast from
Vancouver to Baja California.

Comments: Both the adults and
larvae feed on the roots and leaves of
sea sandwort. The long hairs along the
edge of the body and on the legs help the
adults maneuver in the sand. A parasitic fly (*Reinhardiana petiolata*: Diptera:
Tachinidae) deposits eggs on the beetle
larva (top center). When the eggs hatch,
the fly maggots enter and consume the
beetle larva. After killing their host, the
maggots form puparia inside the dead
insect.

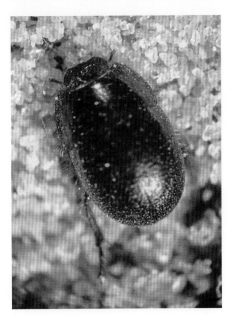

PINK SAND VERBENA

Three species of sand verbena occur along the Pacific coast. The most common is the yellow-flowered species that grows in the dunes. The pink sand verbena is a rare annual that appears at the top of the strand. The pink floral structures in the delicate flower heads are really sepals, because petals are absent. The dark green leaves are thick, leathery, and sticky, which accounts for the adhering sand particles. Thousands of tiny papillae on the leaf surface exude minuscule drops of viscous material that trap small insects, along with sand grains. Some seed bugs find refuge under the prostrate leaves.

A delicate fragrance emanates from the flower clusters of pink sand verbena and is best detected on calm mornings before wind velocity increases. Bumblebees and kelp flies visit the flowers at this time. Flowers offer refuge and food for thrips, which are attacked by small predatory rove beetles, which are in turn parasitized by nematodes. Pink sand verbena flowers also attract the elusive sand dune weevils that come out at night to feed. At dusk, deer browse on its leaves.

Sand caterpillars do the most damage to the plants. These caterpillars rest beneath the sand during the day, nibbling on the roots, and venture forth at night to feed on the leaves and stems. They don't hesitate to use their powerful mandibles to fend off attacks by ground beetles. Many caterpillars are injured in these combats and usually die later from bacterial infections. Others acquire viral infections, become lethargic, and die.

The woodland skipper and red admiral butterfly commonly visit the flowers of pink sand verbena for pollen and nectar, even though their caterpillars develop on other dune plants.

PINK SAND VERBENA COMMUNITY		
Herbivores	Predators	Parasites
Seed bug	American crow	Virus
Sand dune weevil	Rove beetles	Nematode
Red admiral butterfly	Snowy plover	
Sand caterpillar		
Thrip		
Bumblebees		
Kelp fly		
White-tailed deer		
Woodland skipper		

Pink sand verbena is becoming rare in the northern part of its range. It is curious that the western snowy plover, which uses the foliage of pink sand verbena as a protective cover for its eggs and young, is now considered a threatened species.

PINK SAND VERBENA
(*Abronia umbellata*: Nyctaginaceae)
Characteristics: Annual or short-lived perennial with slender, fleshy, branched, prostrate stems; leaves glandular, oval to elliptical with irregular borders; flowers pink, with four or five united sepal lobes (petals absent), four or five stamens, and three styles; pods deeply lobed or winged.
Habitat and range: Coastal strands and dunes, mostly in California, but has appeared as far north as British Columbia.
Comments: Pink sand verbena blooms from June to September along the Oregon and California coasts where the seedpods are washed far enough up the beach for the seedlings to escape subsequent high tides. In California where winds have blown the seeds above the strand line, plants can survive for several years.

SEED BUG
(Hemiptera: Lygaeidae)
Characteristics: Small brown bug with ocelli, dark spots on the head and thorax, and slender legs and antennae.
Habitat and range: Seed bugs are widespread along the Pacific coast.
Comments: Several species of seed bug feed on pink sand verbena.

SAND DUNE WEEVIL

(*Trigonoscuta pilosa*: Coleoptera: Curculionidae)

Characteristics: Mature eggs are black and hatchlings light yellow. Adults are small, short-snouted brown beetles covered with white scales and scattered long hairs.

Habitat and range: Occurs along the entire Pacific Northwest coast.

Comments: There are several species of dune weevil that closely resemble each other. The adults hide during the day and feed at night. All are well camouflaged against the sand and deposit their eggs near the roots of host plants.

RED ADMIRAL BUTTERFLY

(*Vanessa atalanta*: Lepidoptera: Nymphalidae)

Characteristics: Large brown butterfly with a broad orange band across the forewings and across the outer margins of the hind wings. Tips of forewings with white spots.

Habitat and range: All along the Pacific coast and elsewhere.

Comments: Red admiral butterflies visit pink sand verbena for nectar and pollen. The caterpillars develop on various plants in the nettle family.

SAND CATERPILLAR

(*Lasionycta* spp.: Lepidoptera: Noctuidae)

Characteristics: Midsized caterpillars of varying shades of brown to green, often with three to seven partially broken lighter bands extending the length of the body. Pupae brown, broad, formed in the sand. Adult moths midsized, grayish to brownish, with wings bearing some darker markings.

Habitat and range: All along the Pacific coast.

Comments: This genus occurs worldwide and several species can be found along the Pacific coast. Some of the caterpillars are infected by a nuclear polyhedrosis virus (NPV; Baculoviridae). Infected individuals are smaller, darker, and less active than healthy caterpillars. Their integument ruptures soon after death, releasing the infective inclusion bodies into the environment.

ORACHE

Orache, or saltbush, sends its stems along the surface of the sand in the upper strand searching for optimum sun exposure and wind protection. It is easy to overlook the small, green to reddish flower clusters that form at the stem tips. When young, the leaves are covered with a powdery white bloom that disappears as the plant matures, resulting in hairless, triangular, dark green leaves that are often tinged with red. People often collect these for salads and other dishes.

When orache appears late in the season, it must mature and produce seeds before the fall storms sweep the plants away into the ocean. The timing of the seeds' germination makes the difference between life and death, not only for themselves but also for their herbivores. Even before the triangular leaves have completely opened, they are detected by a leaf-mining fly that has its own timetable. The timing of the adult fly's exit from last year's puparium to mate and oviposit eggs so the hatching larvae can enter the leaves of an orache plant is another life-and-death decision. If too early, orache may not yet have formed its leaves. If too late, the plant may already be dying, another herbivore may have eaten the leaves, or a fungus may have made the plant unpalatable.

After hatching, the white fly maggot penetrates the top surface of the leaf and begins to consume the soft tissues between the epidermal layers. Feeding inside the leaf affords protection from wind, rain, and predators. The maggot doesn't appear to be bothered by having its home constantly twisted and flapped around by the wind. It usually consumes the entire inner leaf tissues before dropping to the ground and forming a puparium.

At about the same time the flies appear, orache plants are attacked by zebra moth caterpillars. Aside from their red heads, these colorful caterpillars actually have some zebra-like patterns in the bold horizontal yellow lines that border vertical white stripes against a black background. Their bright hues contrast sharply with the drab tan of the moths that emerge from the pupal cases. The caterpillars feed quite rapidly while they are completely exposed on the leaves, yet I never saw them being targeted by birds other than a few white-crowned sparrows.

Another, much smaller caterpillar feeds on the reddish seed heads. These seed-head caterpillars are well concealed and actually bind the seed clusters with webbing to make their abode more secure. Even though they are much smaller than the zebra caterpillars and have protective coloration, they remain partially hidden among the seed clusters. They have good reason to be secretive: parasitic wasps search them out, in many cases successfully. Those caterpillars that escape the wasps form a tan pupa within the flower heads. The emerging small, dark-speckled brown moths blend in perfectly when resting on orache stems. It is interesting how all three insect herbivores on orache have partitioned the plant so that none interferes with the feeding activities of the others.

ORACHE COMMUNITY		
Herbivores	Predators	Parasites
Leaf-mining fly	Birds	Parasitic wasps
Zebra moth		
Seed-head moth		

ORACHE
(*Atriplex patula*: Amaranthaceae)
Characteristics: Small, prostrate to upright annual with branched stems and fleshy, triangular or arrow-shaped, green to reddish leaves, which sometimes have a powdery white covering. Flowers inconspicuous, present June–November, green to reddish, with separate male and female flowers borne on spikelets at tips of stems or in leaf axils; seeds develop in fleshy, triangular red bracts.
Habitat and range: Coastal strands, dunes, tidal marshes from Alaska through most of California; also along Atlantic coast and on inland saline or alkaline soils in North America and Europe.
Comments: Orache is more common in the northern part of its range, but I have observed plants as far south as Morro Bay, California. The plants grow rapidly in summer and fall when the prevailing winds change from north to south and the ensuing warm, calm period provides optimum growing conditions.

LEAF-MINING FLY

(*Pegomyia betae*: Diptera: Anthomyiidae)

Characteristics: The small white maggots that mine the leaves have round tails and pointed heads that bear a pair of dark mouth hooks. The reddish-tan puparia are elliptical and form in the leaves or in sand near the base of the plant. Adult flies are small and grayish, with a partial dark longitudinal line on the midthorax, and large reddish eyes.

Habitat and range: Coastal areas from Washington to California.

Comments: This is the most widespread herbivore on orache along the coast, and populations can build up and destroy entire plants in late summer.

ZEBRA MOTH

(*Melanchra picta*: Lepidoptera: Noctuidae)

Characteristics: Caterpillars large and black, with a red head and three to five longitudinal yellow lines bordering numerous white cross lines. The pupae are large, robust, and deep reddish brown. Adult moths are reddish brown and have a reflexed head and some white markings on the wings. The thorax is covered with a thick layer of long scales.

Habitat and range: Along the entire Pacific coast as well as throughout inland areas in northwestern North America.

Comments: The striking caterpillars are diurnal leaf feeders that roll up and fall to the ground when disturbed.

SEED-HEAD MOTH

(*Aroga* sp.: Lepidoptera: Gelechiidae)

Characteristics: Caterpillar small, tan to gray, body with three light brownish horizontal lines and a series of brown spots surrounded by halos. Pupa small, brown, formed in flower head. Adult moth small, brown, and slender, with black, brown, and tan patches on forewings.

Habitat and range: Along the strand in Washington and Oregon.

Comments: The caterpillars feed on the developing seeds.

NEW ZEALAND SPINACH

When I search for newly established plants along the strand, every day brings some surprises. One fine spring morning, a cluster of triangular fleshy leaves caught my attention. The leaf surfaces were covered with tiny, almost microscopic "bumps." I then recognized this emergent sprout as New Zealand spinach, a drifter that originates from the Southern Hemisphere, presumably around New Zealand and Australia.

The small, inconspicuous, yellowish-green flowers occur in the leaf axils. The developing ovary is covered with the same minute projections that occur on the leaves. Under the microscope, these structures look like jelly-filled spheres. Their role is a mystery, but they could buffer wind-borne sand particles and keep them from damaging the plant, or perhaps they store water or excess salt. As the name "New Zealand spinach" implies, its young leaves are eaten (preferably cooked) throughout much of its range. A few bites will verify that the leaves are definitely salty. I encountered this plant growing on the strand on only a few occasions. I found some caterpillars, presumably generalist feeders, on the leaves.

NEW ZEALAND SPINACH COMMUNITY
Herbivores
Caterpillar

NEW ZEALAND SPINACH

(*Tetragonia tetragonioides*: Aizoaceae)

Characteristics: Annual to biennial herb
with branching, decumbent stems; leaves
somewhat fleshy, ovate to triangular, entire to slightly lobed, covered with minute
bladder-like glands; flowers unisexual,
yellowish, petals absent; stamens ten
to twenty; styles three to eight, mostly
solitary in leaf axils; fruit four-angled,
with four to ten seeds.

Habitat and range: Coastal strands,
dunes, stony beaches from Oregon to
San Francisco Bay. The native home of
New Zealand spinach is not known, but it
occurs along the coasts of New Zealand,
Australia, Tasmania, Pacific Islands, Japan,
and South America.

Comments: Small, slender, brownish-
green caterpillars (Lepidoptera:
Tortricidae) of an unknown moth feed
on the leaves. When the seeds of New
Zealand spinach germinate slightly beyond
the tide level, they quickly develop a
cluster of leafy stems.

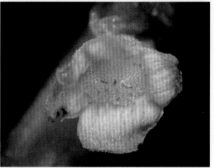

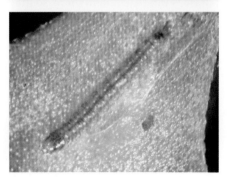

SEASIDE DOCK

The fate of plants and their associates living in an unstable habitat like the strand is uncertain. Not only winter storms but also high tides can remove the community anytime. Perhaps that is why strand plants like seaside dock grow so quickly. In April or May, clusters of green leaves spring up from the basal rosettes, followed a few days later by the flower heads, which quickly open and expose their minute petals. By early fall the flower clusters of seaside dock begin to turn from greenish to a vibrant scarlet, in contrast to the slender deep-green leaves. The small, densely clustered, circular green fruits harden into a mass of minute, rigid red spheres. Eventually the combined weight of the seed heads forces many of the stems against the sand, where they provide an excellent refuge for small intertidal insects and dwarf spiders.

Slender sawfly larvae blend in with the leaves of seaside dock perfectly, and they remain immobile when disturbed, which makes them even harder to detect. When finished feeding, the larvae form delicate green pupae at the base of the plant, completely unprotected. Those that survive change into active black adults.

Brown patches on some seaside dock leaves represent a viscous deposit covering a very strange beetle larva with an extremely small head and barely detectable legs. This little brown larva transforms into a pale, soft pupa that in turn matures into a shiny, oval adult beetle with a reticulated pattern of brown spots on its wing covers. It is unusual to find such a water scavenger beetle feeding on plant leaves.

The inconspicuous flowers of seaside dock don't escape the notice of fly maggots that find a home among the tightly bound flower clusters. Few predators or parasites can reach them there, so they can develop in relative peace. Black aphids that form dense colonies on the stems of seaside dock in the spring are more obvious. The parthenogenetic females are able to increase their numbers very quickly. Occasionally, purplish copper butterflies lay eggs on the leaves of seaside dock. The stubby green caterpillars are well camouflaged and almost impossible to detect. This entire seaside dock community disappears with the arrival of the first November storms, which often eradicate entire plants overnight.

SEASIDE DOCK COMMUNITY		
Herbivores	Predators	Use for shelter
Sawfly	Dwarf spider	Amphipods
Water scavenger beetle		Springtails
Black aphid		Shore bugs
Flower-head maggot		

SEASIDE DOCK

(*Rumex fueginus*: Polygonaceae)

Characteristics: Annual or biennial with fleshy, upright to prostrate reddish stems; leaves mostly basal, elongated, with crisped margins; flowers small, pale green, clustered at tips of stems or in leaf axils, bloom from May to September; fruits spherical, reddish, three-sided, in dense clusters that often lie on the sand.

Habitat and range: Coastal strands, dunes, tidal marshes from British Columbia to California.

Comments: The color difference between the greenish flowers and reddish fruits is quite striking.

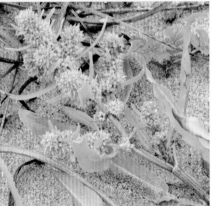

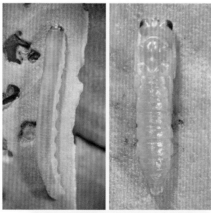

SAWFLY

(*Ametastegia* sp.: Hymenoptera: Tenthredinidae)

Characteristics: Larvae small, green, elongated, with minute white dots on the back. Head light brown, with two dark brown eyespots. Newly formed pupae small, with cream-colored head and thorax and bright green abdomen. Adults black with orange legs.

Habitat and range: Occurs along the coast from Washington to California.

Comments: The green of the larvae is almost identical to the leaf color, making the larvae nearly impossible to detect.

DWARF SPIDER

(*Erigone* sp.: Araneae: Linyphiidae)

Characteristics: Small brownish spider with a smooth, shiny body; legs with three claws.

Habitat and range: Found along the shore including under the leaves of plants such as seaside dock.

Comments: These spiders make small sheet webs. Their egg sacs, which are often attached to driftwood and plant stems, are flat with a raised center and resemble fried eggs.

 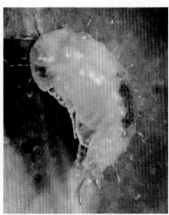 

WATER SCAVENGER BEETLE
(*Laccobius* sp.: Coleoptera: Hydrophilidae)

Characteristics: Larva small, robust, brown, somewhat flattened, with very short legs and small head. Pupa small, cream colored, curved ventrally. Adult small, oval, shiny, with head and pronotum dark, yellow wing covers with rows of brown dots and some dark blotches.

Habitat and range: Top of the strand in Oregon.

Comments: It is unusual for a member of this beetle family to develop on leaves. They normally develop in aquatic habitats.

BLACK APHID
(*Aphis* sp.: Hemiptera: Aphididae)

Characteristics: A small, robust black aphid with short cornicles.

Habitat and range: Thus far, recovered only in Oregon.

Comments: These aphids occur in small but dense groups on the stems of seaside dock.

FLOWER-HEAD MAGGOT
(Diptera: Anthomyiidae)

Characteristics: Small, tubular, legless white maggot with head bearing short, pointed mouth hooks. Adult not found. **Habitat and range:** Dune areas from Washington to California. **Comments:** The maggots feed on the developing seeds.

BRASS BUTTONS

The bright yellow flowers of brass buttons stand out along the beach from March through December. They look like beacons against the dark sand, stiffly bobbing in the breeze. The compact round blossoms appear remarkably similar to buttons and contrast against the fleshy green leaves. The plants often occur in clusters along the strand or in seepage areas where water from sand banks slowly flows into the sea. Those growing along the strand line rarely survive the winter storms and can be considered annuals, but in seepage areas brass buttons reappears at the same spot year after year.

Aside from some butterfly visitors to the flowers, I found only a single insect feeding on brass buttons. Its strong aroma and bitter taste could be offensive to herbivores. Nevertheless, clusters of green aphids feed on the stems, slowly waving their long antennae. A few even perch on the flowers. The long, straight tubes, or cornicles, protruding from the abdomen of the adults serve as a deterrent to predators and parasites by producing a defensive fluid.

BRASS BUTTONS COMMUNITY
Herbivores
Brass buttons aphid
Butterflies

BRASS BUTTONS
(*Cotula coronopifolia*: Asteraceae)
Characteristics: An upright to semidecumbent annual or perennial with strong-scented, leafy stems and alternate, sessile, elliptical leaves with entire or toothed margins and sheathing bases. Flowers composed only of compact yellow disk florets borne singly on terminal peduncles; fruits (achenes) flattened, winged, lacking hairs.
Habitat and range: Coastal strands and tidal marshes from Vancouver Island to California.
Comments: Along the shore, brass buttons functions as an annual, being washed away by winter storms. However, farther inland and in seepage areas, it can be perennial. This is one of the earliest (March) and latest (December) strand plants to flower. Brass buttons was introduced from South Africa and, though considered an exotic, is now widely distributed along the Pacific coast.

BRASS BUTTONS APHID

(Hemiptera: Aphididae)

Characteristics: Small, light green aphids with dark eyes, long antennae, and very long, thin cornicles.

Habitat and range: Thus far, found only along the Oregon coast.

Comments: Most aphids cluster on the stems, but a few feed on the flowers. The long cornicles are thought to emit defensive compounds that deter enemies.

DUNE PLANT COMMUNITIES

Dunes are large areas of windblown sand, sometimes in the form of hills and gullies. Dunes along the Pacific coast have much in common with inland dunes. There are few nutrients and very little available freshwater, and the surface is constantly assailed by wind-borne sand particles. In the summer, the surface of the sand can reach 120°F, while at night, cool fog covers the surface. While it may be difficult to envision anything surviving in such an environment, coastal sand dunes abound with life forms, from minute microbes to flowering plants. Many of their lives are intertwined in ways we can't even begin to comprehend.

Traditionally, coastal dunes have been characterized in many ways. They are usually separated into vegetative regions based on their distance from the ocean. Foredunes extend from the end of the strand to the first perennial herbaceous plants. Middunes extend from the end of the foredunes to the first perennial shrubs. Back dunes extend from the perennial shrub region to the first dwarf trees, which may merge with taller trees and eventually form dune forests. Within these dune regions may occur deflation plains (lower areas) and/or hammocks (sand mounds). Dune formations are quite variable and differ in the length of the various regions and in the types of plants encountered. In fact, every dune system along the Pacific coast is different and has its own unique physical characteristics.

While there are still a few dune areas where bare sand dominates the landscape, the physical features of Pacific coast dune systems changed dramatically at the turn of the nineteenth century with the introduction of marram or beach grass. This grass from Europe and the Eastern Seaboard was intentionally planted all along the Pacific coast in an effort to stabilize the dunes. Now, instead of the dunes representing a constantly shifting landscape, they are fairly uniform. While beach grass has made it possible to construct buildings along the coast, it is crowding out previously established plants, especially the natives.

In all established ecosystems, the adapted organisms have reached a balance and formed an equilibrium. When a new organism is introduced into the system, especially an aggressive one like beach grass, the balance changes and the results can be chaotic. Eventually, a new ecosystem is established, but rarely does this occur without the loss of organisms that were part of the original habitat. As dune plants disappear, so do many of their animal associates that existed in this precarious environment.

Dune plants and their associated biota along the Pacific coast are portrayed in the following pages. Both native and introduced plants that occur in the Pacific coastal environment are included. Some plants profiled here can be considered keystone species because they provide food and shelter for an assortment of dependent life forms. How much longer these associations will exist is difficult to say, but with new construction and increased human recreational activity along the Pacific coast, many of them will probably disappear within the century.

MARRAM GRASS

Marram grass was introduced from Europe and eastern North America as a strand stabilizer along the Pacific coast. Marram grass is well suited to a coastal environment because it has the ability to roll or fold its leaves inward when exposed to heat or high winds, thus conserving water. But by and large, the most significant feature that enables its survival by the sea lies below the ground. Marram grass forms an extensive subterranean system of rhizomes and roots that can establish a network twenty feet deep.

Around the roots flourish species of mycorrhizal fungi that form symbiotic relationships with marram grass, transferring phosphorus, macronutrients, trace elements, and water to the plant in return for carbon. Marram grass has also formed a symbiotic association with bacteria that reside within the cell walls of its stems and rhizomes. The bacteria fix nitrogen, which is probably the single most important nutrient that limits plant growth in nutrient-poor sand.

Early in the morning or late in the evening, deer visit the dunes to browse on the plants. Some nibble the leaves of marram grass, but they don't linger for long. A green stink bug that looks like an old copper-stained penny with a few rust marks on its back can be found sucking sap from the leaves. Hairy caterpillars of the ctenucha moth consume the leaves. The black adult moths with their red heads and shoulder patches stand out against the light green leaves. The large grubs of the ten-lined june beetle develop on the roots. Some grubs never reach adulthood and fall prey to a fungus. Armored darkling beetles laboriously moving over the surface of the sand appear to be easy targets for predators. However, when threatened, the beetle lowers its head and emits a foul-smelling liquid from its anus. This mode of defense is obviously successful, since the beetles still patrol the dunes at midday.

The seeds of marram grass mature in late July and August, but in some instances, instead of normal seeds, the flowers produce elongated, dark, hard fungal bodies called ergots. The fungus replaces the seed with its own tissue and then produces spores in a sweet deposit that is transported by visiting insects. Some mycorrhizal fungi that form fruiting bodies with marram grass appear as mushrooms on the surface of the sand. One such fungus is the dune cup. Dune cups suddenly appear overnight in wet sand with only their tips protruding. When the sand dries and is blown away, the entire cup is revealed.

When ecologists realized that marram grass was displacing native plants, they initiated dune restoration projects. Within several years after the removal of marram grass, the native flora began to reappear. However, removing marram grass is costly, and without constant attention, the dunes are quickly reinvaded.

MARRAM GRASS COMMUNITY		
Herbivores	Parasites/Pathogens	Symbionts
White-tailed deer	Cordyceps fungus	Dune cup
Stink bug	Deer ked	
Ctenucha moth	Wood tick	
Ten-lined june beetle	Ergot fungus	
Armored darkling beetle		

MARRAM GRASS

(*Ammophila arenaria* and *A. breviligulata*: Poaceae)

Characteristics: Coarse perennial grass with narrow, stiff, sharp-pointed leaves and multiple deep rhizomes that spread rapidly through the sand. Flowers borne in dense, terminal, yellow to tan spikes from May to June.

Habitat and range: Now established all along the Pacific coast to stabilize the sand dunes.

Comments: Marram grass is very aggressive and replaces native dune plants.

WHITE-TAILED DEER

(*Odocoileus virginianus*: Cervidae)
Characteristics: Body tan in summer, grayish brown in winter, with a large dark tail that is whitish beneath. The fawn is spotted. Antlers are shed annually.
Habitat and range: Throughout North America in woods, fields, and other habitats.
Comments: Travels alone or in small family units. These deer are browsers, feeding on a variety of plants as well as mushrooms, acorns, and so forth. The deer carry parasites, such as deer keds and ticks, which are capable of transmitting pathogens to humans.

DEER KED

(*Lipoptena* sp.: Diptera: Hippoboscidae)
Characteristics: A small fly with a flattened body, wide head, huge legs, and a pair of broad wings that extend some distance behind the body.
Habitat and range: Occurs along the coast from Washington to California and elsewhere.
Comments: After landing on a deer, the fly sheds its wings and burrows through the hair to reach the deer's skin, where it sucks blood. It is also known to bite humans.

WOOD TICK

(*Dermacentor variabilis*: Arachnida: Ixodidae)
Characteristics: A small brown tick with a white back speckled with brown spots and a marginal band of small, alternating light and dark bars.
Habitat and range: Occurs along the coast from Washington to California and elsewhere.
Comments: These ticks are known to carry a range of disease-causing pathogens that can be transferred to humans.

STINK BUG

(*Chlorochroa uhleri*: Hemiptera: Pentatomidae)

Characteristics: The nymphs are small and green and usually have two or more short transverse marks on their abdomen. Adults vary in color but are usually some shade of green.

Habitat and range: Occurs in various habitats in western North America.

Comments: This stink bug feeds on several grasses in the dunes.

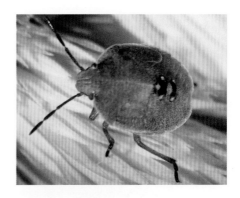

CTENUCHA MOTH

(*Ctenucha multifaria*: Lepidoptera: Arctiidae)

Characteristics: A midsized moth with a red head and shoulder bands, black wings that sometimes have faint whitish tips, and a blue abdomen. The caterpillars are covered with spiny gray hairs, with two tufts of black hair at each end of the body.

Habitat and range: Dunes in Oregon and California and elsewhere.

Comments: Ctenucha caterpillars feed on other grasses besides marram grass.

TEN-LINED JUNE BEETLE

(*Polyphylla decemlineata*: Coleoptera: Scarabaeidae)

Characteristics: The large white grubs are C-shaped and have tan heads. Adults are very large, dark brown beetles with reddish-brown legs and antennae and longitudinal white lines on the thorax and wing covers.

Habitat and range: They occur along the Pacific coast and in other habitats throughout the western states.

Comments: The grubs feed on the roots of marram grass as well as those of beach strawberry and other plants. They are sometimes killed by a fungus (*Cordyceps* sp.) that produces antler-like outgrowths on the victim. Males (on right in photo) have enlarged antennae. Various vertebrates, including coyotes and rodents, feed on the adults.

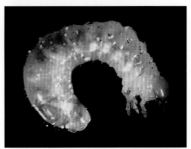

ARMORED DARKLING BEETLE

(*Eleodes suturalis*: Coleoptera: Tenebrionidae)

Characteristics: Midsized black beetle with extremely thick and protective body covering. Head relatively small, with straight, bead-like antennae. Wing covers with rows of small tubercles. Pronotum flattened at margins, with small basal corner projections.

Habitat and range: Occurs among clumps of marram grass and on open sand in Oregon and California along the coast.

Comments: In spite of its black color, this beetle often occurs in full sunlight on the surface of the sand. The larvae feed on grass roots and the adults are detritivores.

ERGOT

(*Claviceps purpurea*: Agaricales: Clavariaceae)

Characteristics: Elongated, dark fungal fruiting bodies (ergots) emerging among the grass kernels are characteristic of the disease. These fruiting bodies produce drops containing numerous conidia that spread the pathogen.

Habitat and range: Global, but prefers hot, humid climates.

Comments: Ingestion of ergot can result in a disease known as ergotism.

DUNE CUP

(*Sarcosphaera [Peziza] ammophila*: Pezizales: Pezizaceae)

Characteristics: A fungus with a cup-shaped brown fruiting body that develops underground with only the top protruding from the sand. Margin deeply lobed, outer wall thick, brittle, and sand encrusted, eventually splitting into segments.

Habitat and range: Dunes from Washington to California and elsewhere.

Comments: Dune cups are usually solitary, but two or three can occur together. They are difficult to detect because they are small, grow partially concealed in the sand, and don't remain for long periods.

AMERICAN DUNE GRASS

Before the arrival of marram grass, American dune grass was the main grass of the lower dunes and occasionally of the upper strand. It is obvious that marram grass has displaced American dune grass in many areas, probably because of its massive root system. Sand dune moths lay rows of pearly eggs on the underside of the leaves of American dune grass. These hatch into yellowish-brown caterpillars that have no difficulty digesting the tough leaves, and they remain on the plant for a time. When they are larger, they drop and burrow into the sand during the day, come out in the evening to feed, and then retreat into the sand again during the day. The pupa forms in the sand, and a strikingly patterned brown moth emerges, quite a contrast to the greasy-looking sand caterpillar. Occasionally, instead of a moth, a robust fly appears. The maggot of this parasite forms its puparium inside the caterpillar's pupa.

Tiny gall gnat maggots develop inside the softer leaf tissues, with the outer layers serving as a protective shield. The maggots eat rapidly, leaving behind yellow patches devoid of chlorophyll. In their brown puparia, they change from yellowish larvae to small gray flies. Spotted-wing grasshoppers that breed inland migrate down to the coastal areas to locate American dune grass. They feed alone or in small groups and are quick to fly, and thus difficult to catch by hand. American dune grass, like marram grass, is also susceptible to ergot fungi.

AMERICAN DUNE GRASS COMMUNITY	
Herbivores	Parasites
Dune cutworm	Bee fly
Gall gnat	Ergot fungus
Spotted-wing grasshopper	

AMERICAN DUNE GRASS

(*Leymus mollis*: Poaceae)
Characteristics: Wide-leaved perennial grass with dense, soft, terminal flower spikes.
Habitat and range: Dunes from Alaska to California.
Comments: American dune grass did not survive well after the introduction of marram grass and occurs as single or small groups of plants, often in areas suboptimal for the growth of marram grass. The flowering spikelets appear in May and June.

DUNE CUTWORM

(*Euxoa* sp.: Lepidoptera: Noctuidae)

Characteristics: Eggs pale and oval, deposited in rows on grass stems. Early larval stages pale, with a reddish back and tan head capsule. Later larval stages pale gray, with a green line running down the back. Adult moths very large, brown, with three light oval marks on the forewings.

Habitat and range: I found this cutworm feeding only on American dune grass in Oregon.

Comments: The young caterpillars remain on the plant, while the older ones bury themselves in the sand during the day and feed at night. This is one of several noctuid cutworms known as "sand caterpillars."

BEE FLY

(*Villa* sp.: Diptera: Bombyliidae)

Characteristics: Robust, midsized brown fly with a large round head, short antennae, large tan eyes that almost meet at the top of the head, clear wings, and slender legs.

Habitat and range: The genus is widespread throughout the dune system.

Comments: Larvae of this fly genus parasitize various cutworms.

ERGOT
(*Claviceps purpurea*: Agaricales: Clavariaceae)
Characteristics: Elongated, dark fungal fruiting bodies (ergots) within the grass kernels are characteristic of the disease.
Habitat and range: Global, including dune habitats.
Comments: Other dune grasses, including marram grass, are also infected by this fungus.

GALL GNAT
(Diptera: Cecidomyiidae)
Characteristics: Larva small, legless; pupa small, ringed, orange. Adult fly small, black, delicate, with long legs.
Habitat and range: Thus far, found only on American dune grass in Oregon.
Comments: The larvae develop within the leaves, and occasionally in the stems.

SPOTTED-WING GRASSHOPPER
(*Camnula pellucida*: Orthoptera: Acrididae)
Characteristics: A midsized yellowish-brown grasshopper with large eyes, short antennae, reddish pronotum and hind femur, and dark spots on outer wings (tegmina).
Habitat and range: From Canada to California along the coast and also inland.
Comments: There are several color variations of this little grasshopper. They occur singly or in small groups.

TUFTED HAIR GRASS

The dunes contain many grasses, including introduced species like orchard grass and sweet vernal grass, but most are not dominant along the coast. One native grass that occurs in deflation plains is tufted hair grass. It has tufted narrow leaves and reddish-purple spikelets (flower heads) that nod in the breeze and provide a unique background to the spring landscape.

Small grass moths whose caterpillars feed on tufted hair grass and other dune grasses have striking wing patterns that may assist the moths in moving among the spikelets without detection.

Several types of grasshopper frequent the dunes and feed on tufted hair grass. One of these is the notched-neck grasshopper, so named because it has a notch on the top of the pronotum directly behind its head. The adults are strong fliers and are well camouflaged when resting on the sand. Minute pygmy grasshoppers also feed on tufted hair grass. The nymphs are able to change their body colors to match that of the substrate and are almost impossible to detect.

Yellow slime molds grow on the surfaces of leaves, including those of tufted hair grass. These slime molds appear after rainy periods, and the small droplets of slime may cover the entire surface of the lower leaves. How they move and respond to various stimuli is a mystery.

TUFTED HAIR GRASS COMMUNITY	
Herbivores	Symbionts
Grass moth	Yellow slime mold
Notched-neck grasshopper	
Pygmy grasshopper	

TUFTED HAIR GRASS

(*Deschampsia caespitosa* var. *longiflora*: Poaceae)

Characteristics: Narrow-leaved, tufted perennial with many stems bearing fine, hairlike flowers. Flowers purple, each with two florets. Outer floret parts (glumes) lacking awns; inner floret parts (lemmas) with short awns attached below the middle.

Habitat and range: Washington to California along the coast.

Comments: This particular variety of hair grass occurs along the Pacific coast in dunes and other saline habitats. Flowering occurs from May to July.

GRASS MOTH

(*Diploschizia impigritella*: Lepidoptera: Glyphipterigidae)

Characteristics: A small brown moth with narrow wings fringed at the tips. Forewings with several white lines.

Habitat and range: Washington to California along the Pacific coast and elsewhere in North America.

Comments: The caterpillars develop in the flowering stems and occasionally in the flower clusters.

NOTCHED-NECK GRASSHOPPER

(*Dissosteira pictipennis*: Orthoptera: Acrididae)

Characteristics: A very large, grayish-brown grasshopper with a rosy sheen and a deep notch at the top of the pronotum. The spotted forewings extend beyond the body.

Habitat and range: Dunes and other areas in California and Oregon.

Comments: This grasshopper is a strong flier.

PYGMY GRASSHOPPER

(*Paratettrix* sp.: Orthoptera: Tetrigidae)

Characteristics: A small grasshopper with the thorax extended over the back, usually well over the abdomen. Nymphs dark brown (photo), with protruding round eyes and a V-shaped pronotum with a notched margin.

Habitat and range: Washington to California along the Pacific coast.

Comments: The wingless nymphs are well camouflaged against the damp sand.

YELLOW SLIME MOLD

(*Physarum polycephalum*: Mycetozoa: Physaridae)

Characteristics: Small, circular yellow slime bodies (plasmodia) that move by contraction and relaxation of their protoplasm.

Habitat and range: Washington to California along the Pacific coast and elsewhere in North America.

Comments: Yellow slime mold moves over the surface of leaves, engulfing and digesting microbes. Leaves turn yellow if covered for extended periods, but the slime mold does not parasitize the plant.

BEACH PEA

With its beautiful purple blooms like raised butterfly wings, the beach pea is a sure sign that spring has arrived. Beach pea is one of the few familiar-looking dune flowers, and gardeners will immediately see the resemblance to sweet peas. One can find caterpillars almost everywhere on this plant. They enter the green seedpods and devour the contents without hesitation. After finishing most of the seeds in the pod, the seedpod caterpillar forms a cocoon in the fall. The cocoon is woven extra thick (then called a hibernaculum) to withstand winter storms, and in the spring, a brown moth emerges that begins the cycle anew. A secure domicile is of prime importance for caterpillar survival, and there are many ways to go about it. Some, like the striped, spotted, and yellow leaf-fold caterpillars, live in a shelter created by folding a beach pea leaf over and cementing the edges with sticky saliva. Although completely hidden from view, the caterpillars may still not be safe from wasp and mite parasites. Some caterpillars that can't hide use camouflage for concealment. That is what the green leaf caterpillar does as it devours the leaves of beach pea during the day. Still others, like the inchworm caterpillar, prefer to dine on the petals of beach pea flowers, rather than the leaves.

A fly maggot develops in a mine it makes as it eats the tissue between the leaf surfaces of beach pea. But the mine does not protect it from attack by parasitic wasps, whose larvae pupate inside the mine after destroying the maggot.

Early in the morning, slugs and snails that were active during the night return to their lairs, leaving behind slime trails on the leaves of beach pea. Their slime would appear to be an effective repellent, yet a number of predators attack these mollusks. Large snail-killing beetles with narrow heads and constricted waists enter their shells to search for them. Some parasitic flies lay their eggs on the snail shells. The hatched maggots then enter the shell and penetrate the snail, eventually killing it and forming a puparium within the shell.

Various molds such as powdery mildew attack the leaves of beach pea, marking their presence with white blotches on the leaves. The flowers of beach pea also attract insects, mostly bees, to sample the nectar and collect pollen. Many bumblebees transport small brown juvenile mites on their bodies. The adult mites feed on microorganisms in the bees' nests.

Beach pea has formed a symbiotic relationship with nitrogen-fixing bacteria (rhizobacteria) that live in nodules on the plant's roots. These bacteria pull nitrogen out of the air and convert it into ammonia, which the plant uses. In turn, beach pea supplies the bacteria with carbohydrates needed for energy. While the plant lives, insects and other herbivores benefit from eating the nitrogen-rich leaves. After the plant dies, the nitrogen inside its tissues is released into the soil to nourish detritivores.

The circumglobal distribution of beach pea can be attributed to the seeds' ability to remain viable in seawater for up to five years. Once they reach shore, the pounding surf scarifies the hard seed coat, priming it for germination. The young plants produce an extensive root system that anchors them in the shifting sands. With its nitrogen-fixing bacteria, saltwater-tolerant seeds, and expansive root system, the beach pea is well adapted for survival in coastal dunes.

BEACH PEA COMMUNITY		
Herbivores	Predators	Parasites/Commensals
Seedpod moth	Snail-killing beetle	Leaf-mining wasp parasites
Inchworm flower caterpillar	Snail-killing fly	Caterpillar mites
Striped leaf-fold moth		Powdery mildew
Spotted leaf-fold caterpillar		Bumblebee mites
Yellow leaf-fold caterpillar		Thrombidiid slug mites
Green leaf caterpillar		Braconid caterpillar wasps
Leaf-mining fly		
Field slug		
Garden snail		
Fuzzy-horned bumblebee		
Sweat bee		

BEACH PEA
(*Lathyrus japonicus*: Fabaceae)
Characteristics: Spreading perennial with glabrous, opposite, pinnate leaflets on twining stems bearing branched tendrils. Flowers reddish purple to blue, borne in small clusters. Seeds (peas) borne in large pods.
Habitat and range: Coastal from Alaska to northern California. Also occurs along the East Coast of North America and temperate coasts of Asia and Europe.
Comments: Beach pea is widespread and can be considered a keystone dune plant species because it supports a variety of organisms. Flowering occurs from early May through fall.

DUNE PLANT COMMUNITIES: BEACH PEA

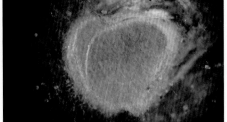

SEEDPOD MOTH

(*Pima* sp.: Lepidoptera: Pyralidae)

Characteristics: Caterpillars midsized, light green with dark green lines running the length of the body. Head and pronotum pale brown. The pupae are formed in silken hibernacula cocoons that overwinter. The midsized adult moths are light brown, with a "snout" and protruding eyes. A dark brown submarginal band runs the length of each forewing.

Habitat and range: Dunes from Washington to California.

Comments: The larvae often destroy most of the seeds before finishing their development.

INCHWORM FLOWER CATERPILLAR

(*Spargania* sp.: Lepidoptera: Geometridae)

Characteristics: Caterpillar large, yellowish, with a grayish-green lateral band extending the length of the body. Only two pairs of prolegs are positioned at the posterior end of the body. Adult moth large, brownish tan, with a black dot near the upper margin of each forewing.

Habitat and range: On beach pea in Oregon and California.

Comments: The caterpillars occur on all parts of the plant, especially the flowers.

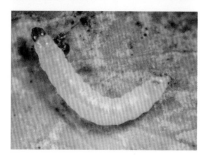

STRIPED LEAF-FOLD MOTH

(*Chionodes* spp.: Lepidoptera: Gelechiidae) and other leaf-fold caterpillars

Characteristics: The striped leaf-fold caterpillar has a dark brown head and pronotum and alternating brown and pale white bands running the length of the body. The adult moth has an oval brown patch on the folded forewings and a curved brown band on the lower half of each forewing.

Habitat and range: On beach pea and gray beach pea from Washington to California.

Comments: I occasionally found two other caterpillars that also glue the edges of two adjacent leaflets together. The spotted leaf-fold caterpillar (top center) has a tan head and is uniformly brown with light circular lumps over its body. The yellow leaf-fold caterpillar (lower photo) is all yellow except for the brown head capsule. Parasitic mites (Acarina: Erythraeidae) and wasps (Hymenoptera: Braconidae) attack the caterpillars.

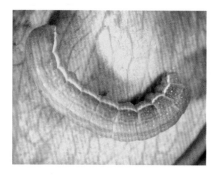

GREEN LEAF CATERPILLAR

(*Dryotype* sp.: Lepidoptera: Noctuidae)

Characteristics: Very large green caterpillar with white dorsal and subdorsal lines running the length of the body. Adults not known.

Habitat and range: Widespread on beach pea in dunes from Washington to California.

Comments: The caterpillars are well camouflaged and feed during the day, usually on the undersides of the leaves.

DUNE PLANT COMMUNITIES: BEACH PEA

LEAF-MINING FLY

(*Amauromyza lathyroides*: Diptera: Agromyzidae)

Characteristics: Larva small, whitish, develops inside blotch mines in the leaves of beach pea. Excreta are deposited as black particles in the mine. Puparium small, brown, formed in the mine. Adult small, gray, with brown eyes, clear wings, dark longitudinal lines on thorax, and pointed abdomen.

Habitat and range: These leaf miners occur on beach pea in California and Oregon.

Comments: Small, white, parasitic wasp larvae (Hymenoptera: Eulophidae) kill the leaf miners and then pupate within the mines.

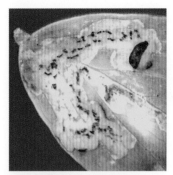

FIELD SLUG

(*Deroceras* sp.: Gastropoda: Agriolimacidae)

Characteristics: A large, light brown slug with dark head and antennae and a reticulate pattern on its back.

Habitat and range: Widespread throughout the dunes from Washington to California.

Comments: These slugs rasp away the surface layers of beach pea leaves. Their presence is revealed by a slime layer on the foliage. Trombidiid mites (Acarina: Trombidiidae) live in the mantle cavity of these slugs.

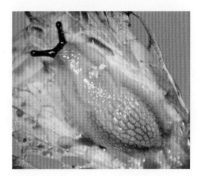

GARDEN SNAIL
(*Helix aspersa*: Gastropoda: Helicidae)
Characteristics: Dark brown snail with broadly coiled shell. Body reticulated, with long antennae bearing small oval "eyes" at the tips.
Habitat and range: Widespread throughout the dunes from Washington to California.
Comments: This Eurasian snail is usually present during the evening and early morning. It is attacked by snail-killing beetles.

SNAIL-KILLING BEETLE
(*Scaphinotus angusticollis*: Coleoptera: Carabidae)
Characteristics: Large black beetle with a narrow, elongated head and pronotum, protruding mouthparts, long and slender legs, and a wide abdomen with a speckled border.
Habitat and range: From Alaska to California in cool, damp localities, especially among the denser vegetation in the back dunes.
Comments: These nocturnal beetles use their powerful jaws to attack snails, reaching into the shells with their constricted foreparts. They also attack slugs. When disturbed, they emit a defensive spray that can burn human skin.

SNAIL-KILLING FLY
(*Sarcophaga* sp.: Diptera: Sarcophagidae)
Characteristics: A small gray fly with red eyes, three wide black longitudinal lines on the thorax, and a few long bristles on the abdomen.
Habitat and range: Throughout the dunes from Washington to California and elsewhere.
Comments: This fly (photo) emerged from a puparium attached to the shell of the snail *Monadenia* sp. (Gastropoda: Monadeniidae). Terrestrial snails in the dunes are associated with various flies, some of which are parasitic, others of which are scavengers.

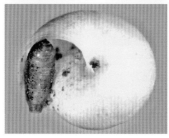

DUNE PLANT COMMUNITIES: BEACH PEA

POWDERY MILDEW

(*Erysiphe* sp.: Fungi: Erysiphaceae)

Characteristics: Colonies of mycelium grow over leaf surfaces, eventually forming white blotches on the leaflets.

Habitat and range: Widespread throughout the dunes from Washington to California.

Comments: Powdery mildews occur on many plants but are the most conspicuous in the dunes on beach pea.

FUZZY-HORNED BUMBLEBEE

(*Bombus mixtus*: Hymenoptera: Apidae)

Characteristics: A midsized bumblebee with yellowish hairs covering most of its body.

Habitat and range: Throughout the dunes from Alaska to northern California and elsewhere.

Comments: This species has a medium-sized tongue and appears early in the spring just after the beach pea flowers open. They frequently carry minute juvenile bumblebee mites (*Kuzinia* sp.: Acarina: Acaridae), which have four legs pointing forward and four pointing backward and are obligate associates of bumblebees. These mites are phoretic and are carried from nest to nest, where they feed on microorganisms.

SWEAT BEE

(*Lasioglossum* sp.: Hymenoptera: Halictidae)

Characteristics: A small, dull metallic black bee with a wide head and yellowish hairs on the sides of the thorax.

Habitat and range: Along the coast from Alaska to northern California and elsewhere.

Comments: These bees are solitary, usually nest in the ground, and carry pollen between the stiff hairs on their hind legs.

BIG-HEADED SEDGE

Big-headed sedge is one of the few sedges found in the lower dunes, where it is subject to intermittent salt spray. It is a coarse plant with thick, leathery leaves and highly protective flower heads. Borne at the tip of a single, short stalk, both the male and female florets, which occur on separate plants, are so stiff and tightly clustered that it is impossible to remove them by hand. A pair of thick leather gloves and pliers are necessary when looking for herbivores in the flower heads of big-headed sedge.

It's a wonder that insects can wiggle their way into these tightly compressed flower clusters, but eventually I discovered some small caterpillars in the female flowers. One reddish-brown caterpillar bores down into the base of the sharp floral bracts and remains there for the course of its development. Green tortricid caterpillars also manage to hide among the flowers but spin a silken web around their new domicile. Elusive leaf caterpillars covered with pepper spots feed among the leaves at the base of the plant and share this habitat with larvae of a leaf-mining fly.

BIG-HEADED SEDGE COMMUNITY
Herbivores
Flower-head caterpillar
Tortricid caterpillar
Leaf caterpillar
Leaf-mining fly

BIG-HEADED SEDGE

(*Carex macrocephala*: Cyperaceae)

Characteristics: Male and female flowers on separate plants. Flowers arranged in tightly bunched, cylindrical heads subtended by large, sharp bracts. Leaves three-ranked, parallel veined, elongated, thick, and tough. Stems triangular in cross section.

Habitat and range: Dunes and adjacent areas from Alaska to Oregon.

Comments: The plants often occur in small groups of two to ten individuals. Flowering occurs in May and June.

FLOWER-HEAD CATERPILLAR

(*Elachista* sp.: Lepidoptera: Elachistidae)

Characteristics: A small, flat, reddish-brown caterpillar with short legs and a pair of pale stripes running the length of the body.

Habitat and range: Dunes in Washington and Oregon.

Comments: The caterpillars bore into the developing female flowers.

TORTRICID CATERPILLAR

(Lepidoptera: Tortricidae)

Characteristics: A small greenish-yellow caterpillar with a tan head capsule.

Habitat and range: Dunes in Washington and Oregon.

Comments: The larvae feed within loose webs they spin in the flower heads.

LEAF CATERPILLAR

(*Crambus* sp.: Lepidoptera: Crambidae)

Characteristics: Small, pale white caterpillar covered with dark spots, each bearing a hair. Head and pronotum black. **Habitat and range:** Dunes in Oregon. **Comments:** These caterpillars feed on the basal leaf clusters.

LEAF-MINING FLY

(Diptera: Lauxaniidae)

Characteristics: Larvae legless, cream colored, with distinctly segmented body and mouth hooks. Adults small, black, with large gray eyes and brownish legs. **Habitat and range:** Oregon dunes. **Comments:** The larvae develop within the tightly appressed leaf bases.

BEACH STRAWBERRY

The fruits of beach strawberry may be reduced in size, but their delicious flavor more than compensates for it. This little plant occurs from Alaska to California and has a very successful method of spreading along the dunes. From the base of each plant grow long, narrow, reddish stems without leaves or flowers. These fast-growing stolons extend in many directions, and eventually a small strawberry plant appears at the tip. After becoming established, it then sends off additional stolons.

Beach strawberry attracts a number of creatures, from white-tailed deer and brush rabbits to the smallest worms. Some, like dune ants, flower moths, and flower caterpillars, visit the blooms just for nectar. However, other caterpillars and flea beetles feast on the leaves. Flea beetle larvae often feed on just the lower surfaces, so their presence is not evident from above. When finished, they drop to the ground and change into bright orange-yellow pupae, which then darken before transforming into shiny bronze adults. Larvae of the click beetle and root weevil devour the roots as they spend their lives in the sand, while the adults feed on the aboveground portions. If the adults of these beetles are detected while nibbling on beach strawberry leaves, each has a unique method of escape. The flea beetle has very thick hind legs that enable it to jump many times its length in a fraction of a second, thus taking it out of the danger zone. While the click beetle can't leap, by using a clicking mechanism involving two opposing thoracic segments, it can propel itself high in the air and out of range of the attacker. Even if it lands on its back, it can "click" again to right itself. The root weevil simply drops to the ground, pulls its legs and beak against its heavy body, and plays dead.

However, the beetles also have enemies that live in the sand. Long, slender stiletto fly larvae move through the sand, often leaving a wavy trail visible from above. They can make short work of any insect larva they encounter. The adult flies enjoy sunbathing, and their yellow-striped bodies can be seen fully exposed on the sand.

Root weevils are the favorite prey of parasitic nematodes that also occur in the sand. It takes only one small nematode to kill a large root weevil. The small infective-stage nematode can detect its prey from some distance away and, after locating it, enters the weevil's gut, bores a hole in the intestinal wall, and enters the victim's body cavity. The beetle's immune system then attempts to encase the intruder with blood cells. That is when the nematode releases the microbes it has been carrying in its own gut, which quickly replicate and overpower the weevil's defenses. Now the nematode grows and reproduces inside the dead insect's body. Since each infective-stage nematode is a hermaphrodite, no mate is required.

That is not the only nematode associated with beach strawberry, since some plant parasites direct their attention to the foliage. One nematode that is equipped with a type of mouth syringe (stylet) releases an enzyme that stimulates the plant to form giant cells, producing a stem gall. The nematode then develops on the nutritious contents in the gall.

Some unusual insects also occur on beach strawberry. Small ensign scale insects that look like miniature armored vehicles suck juices from the plants. Carrion beetles obviously want a change of menu from time to time and select ripe strawberries over their normal diet of refuse or dead matter.

BEACH STRAWBERRY COMMUNITY		
Herbivores	Predators	Parasites
Dune ant	Stiletto fly	Insect nematode
Flower moth		Plant nematode
Flower caterpillar		
Flea beetle		
Click beetle		
Root weevil		
Stem nematode		
Ensign scale		
Carrion beetle		
Brush rabbit		
White-tailed deer		

BEACH STRAWBERRY

(*Fragaria chiloensis*: Rosaceae)
Characteristics: Perennial with short roots and long, leafless stolons. Leaves basal, three-parted, toothed. Flowers in open clusters (cymes), normally with five white or pinkish petals. Fruit a red berry covered with seeds (achenes).
Habitat and range: Coastal areas from Alaska to California and elsewhere.
Comments: This is an aggressive plant that spreads rapidly by runners (stolons). Flowers appear in mid-April and continue through the summer and fall.

DUNE ANT

(*Lasius* sp.: Hymenoptera: Formicidae)

Characteristics: Small, dark brown to tan ant with long antennae.

Habitat and range: Widespread genus with coastal and inland species from Washington to California and elsewhere.

Comments: These small ants search for nectar in beach strawberry flowers and may serve as pollinators. They nest under driftwood or rocks or at the base of dune plants.

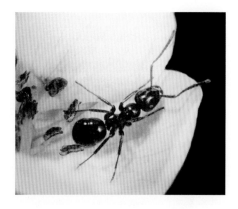

FLOWER MOTH

(*Grapholita* sp.: Lepidoptera: Tortricidae)

Characteristics: Small tan moth with shiny scales. A broad, transverse white band occurs in the middle of each forewing, and there are additional white areas toward the wing tips.

Habitat and range: Found on beach strawberry only in Oregon, but may be widespread.

Comments: These moths take nectar from the flowers. The host plant of the caterpillars is unknown, but it could be one of the dune legumes, since a similar species develops on springbank clover.

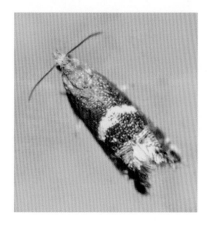

FLOWER CATERPILLAR

(Lepidoptera: Noctuidae)

Characteristics: Light brown caterpillar with three longitudinal reddish lines running the length of the body. Small brown spots occur on the sides of the body.

Habitat and range: Found only on beach strawberry in Oregon but may be widespread.

Comments: This unidentified caterpillar feeds on pollen and other flower parts.

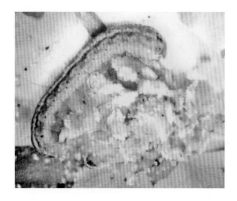

FLEA BEETLE

(*Altica* sp.: Coleoptera: Chrysomelidae)

Characteristics: Larva small, plump, greenish bronze, and covered with small protrusions; pupa small and yellowish orange, with eyes that darken as it matures; adult small, shiny bronze, oblong oval, with antennae half as long as its body. Hind legs adapted for jumping.

Habitat and range: Dunes from Washington to California.

Comments: Mating occurs on the plant soon after adult emergence. The adults are good jumpers.

CLICK BEETLE

(*Limonius* sp.: Coleoptera: Elateridae)

Characteristics: Midsized, smooth, elongated yellowish-brown larvae with short legs and antennae. Shiny, midsized, dark brown beetles covered with scattered pale scales.

Habitat and range: Dunes in Oregon and California.

Comments: The larvae, called wireworms, feed on plant roots, while the adults nibble on the leaves. Pupation occurs in the soil beneath the plant. Predatory larvae of a stiletto fly attack the wireworm larvae.

STILETTO FLY

(*Thereva* sp.: Diptera: Therevidae)

Characteristics: The midsized, elongated, legless yellow larvae superficially resemble click beetle larvae. The midsized adults are slender, with long legs and a narrow abdomen. The body is marked with yellow stripes on the thorax and yellow bands on the abdomen.

Habitat and range: Widespread along the Pacific coast.

Comments: The adults frequently rest on sand during the day. The larvae burrow through the sand looking for prey, which includes click beetle larvae.

ROOT WEEVIL

(*Otiorhynchus* sp.: Coleoptera: Curculionidae)

Characteristics: A midsized, oblong, dark brown snout beetle with fairly long antennae. Elytra with rows of punctures and areas of yellowish scales. Beak short, widened at tip.

Habitat and range: The genus is widespread throughout the Pacific dunes and elsewhere.

Comments: The adults hide during the day and feed at night on the foliage of beach strawberry. Many fall prey to a parasitic nematode.

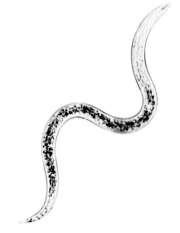

INSECT PARASITIC NEMATODE

(*Heterorhabditis* sp.: Nematoda: Heterorhabditidae)

Characteristics: Infective stage microscopic, elongated, lacking segments, with a minute tooth on the tip of its head. Parasitic adults white, large, reaching half the beetle's length. Eggs and developing juveniles occur in the body cavity of the infected root weevils.

Habitat and range: In dunes along the Pacific Northwest coast.

Comments: The infective stage uses its tooth to enter the body cavity of the insect and then releases specific bacteria (*Photorhabdus luminescens*) carried in its gut. The bacteria kill the insect and provide nutrients for the developing juveniles.

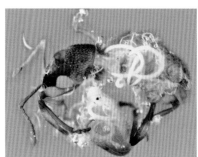

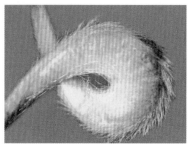

STEM NEMATODE

(*Ditylenchus* sp.: Nematoda: Tylenchidae)

Characteristics: Free-living stage microscopic, slender, with a short mouth stylet. Adults occur only inside galls.

Habitat and range: Widespread along the Pacific coast and elsewhere.

Comments: The nematodes enter the stems of beach strawberry, initiate feeding that stimulates the formation of spiral galls, and complete their life cycle inside the galls.

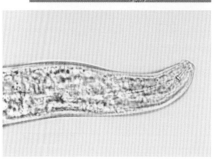

ENSIGN SCALE

(*Newsteadia* sp.: Hemiptera: Ortheziidae)

Characteristics: Small, oval white insects covered with large, waxy white plates. Legs and antennae red, but inconspicuous.

Habitat and range: Found thus far only on beach strawberry in Oregon.

Comments: These scales occur on the underside of leaves and suck up cell sap.

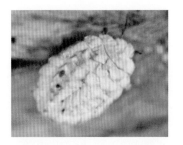

CARRION BEETLE

(*Heterosilpha* sp.: Coleoptera: Silphidae)

Characteristics: Adults large, black, broad and somewhat flat, with a velvety surface. Larvae elongated, shiny black, with overlapping dorsal plates.

Habitat and range: Along the coast from Washington to California.

Comments: While these beetles normally feed on refuse or dead animals, both larvae and adults will also devour strawberries.

GRAY BEACH PEA

Gray beach pea can be difficult to locate because of its grayish-green leaves, especially when it grows among marram grass. It blooms around the first of June, and flower color varies greatly. Usually the blooms are some shade of blue or purple, but violet and even completely white petals can be found, and in some rare instances, both colored and white flowers are encountered on the same plant.

The developing seeds make a meal for seed and pod caterpillars, the latter of which are attacked by parasitic wasps. There are caterpillars that fold over and bind together the edges of the leaves with dense layers of silk, forming a shelter where they remain encased until they are ready to form their cocoons in preparation for the adult stage. Some of these have green stripes, while others have brown stripes. Small brown sand beetles are sometimes found in the pods after the caterpillars have left, and they finish up the leftovers. Quite interesting are the parasitic nematodes inside these beetles. The nematodes appear to cause little harm to the beetles and need to reach the gut of a vertebrate to complete their development, perhaps that of a lizard that feeds on sand beetles.

In some areas gray beach pea is surrounded by the flowering stems of seashore paintbrush. Whether gray beach pea benefits from this association is not known, but seashore paintbrush obtains nutrients from its companion.

GRAY BEACH PEA COMMUNITY	
Herbivores	Parasites
Seed moth	Wasps
Pod moth	Nematodes
Striped leaf-fold caterpillars	Seashore paintbrush
Sand dune beetle	

GRAY BEACH PEA

(*Lathyrus littoralis*: Fabaceae)
Characteristics: Small grayish-green perennial with hairy palmate leaves composed of four to eight leaflets. Stems lack climbing tendrils. Flower color variable, from blue and purple to white. Fruit a hairy pod.
Habitat and range: Dunes from Canada to California.
Comments: Flowering is continuous from late spring through summer. Rarely, white and purple flowers occur on the same plant.

DUNE PLANT COMMUNITIES: GRAY BEACH PEA

SEED MOTH

(*Pima* sp.: Lepidoptera: Pyralidae)

Characteristics: Caterpillars large and light green, with darker green stripes running the length of the body. Head and pronotum tan to gray. Adult moths large, brown, with a "snout" and protruding eyes.

Habitat and range: Dunes in Oregon and California.

Comments: The larvae often destroy most of the seeds before finishing their development, after which they spin a cocoon for pupation.

GREEN- AND BROWN-STRIPED LEAF-FOLD CATERPILLARS

(*Chionodes* spp.: Lepidoptera: Gelechiidae)

Characteristics: Caterpillars midsized, with alternating white and green, brown, or gray stripes extending the length of the body. Head tan on the green-striped caterpillars and dark brown on the brown-striped caterpillars.

Habitat and range: Dunes from Washington to California.

Comments: The caterpillars attach the edges of two adjacent leaflets and develop inside the cavity. A third, unidentified plain caterpillar (Lepidoptera) strips the leaf tips of gray beach pea.

POD MOTH
(*Chionodes* sp.: Lepidoptera: Gelechiidae)
Characteristics: Caterpillar midsized, grayish green with a black head. Adult midsized, rectangular shaped at rest, with forewings light brown and speckled with darker markings.
Habitat and range: Dunes from Washington to California.
Comments: The caterpillars feed on pods as well as on seeds inside the pods. They often move from pod to pod before finishing their development. The mature caterpillar pupates in a loose silken cocoon on the outside of the pod. Wasps (Hymenoptera: Ichneumonidae) that parasitize the caterpillars form a hard, dark pupal case within the pod adjacent to the dead caterpillar.

SAND DUNE BEETLE

(*Phaleria globosa*: Coleoptera: Tenebrionidae)

Characteristics: Small, roundish, light to dark brown beetles with short beaded antennae, often with zigzag lines across the wing covers, and front legs modified for digging. The long, narrow larvae are light brown, with darker ring bands encircling the body segments.
Habitat and range: Dunes from Washington to California.
Comments: These beetles are associated with dune vegetation and scavenge in pods of gray beach pea. The larvae can jump by bending and then quickly straightening their body. Some beetles contain parasitic nematodes (*Physaloptera* sp.: Spirurida) coiled up in their body cavities. These nematodes will develop to maturity only when the beetle is eaten by a vertebrate, which could be a mammal, bird, or reptile.

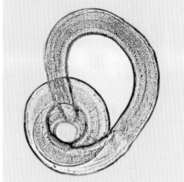

SEASHORE PAINTBRUSH

(*Castilleja exserta* subsp. *latifolia*: Scrophulariaceae)

Characteristics: A semiparasitic, erect perennial with red-tipped flowers surrounded by white bracts, and oblong, usually entire, finely villous leaves.
Habitat and range: Coastal dunes from Washington to Baja California.
Comments: Seashore paintbrush takes nutrients from the roots of gray beach pea.

BEACH SILVER-TOP

Beach silver-top is one of several members of the carrot family that occur in dune habitats and is the only one in which all parts of the plant, including the flower and seed clusters, are closely appressed to the ground. This is the case regardless of whether the plant is growing in coarse black sand in northern California or in fine beach sand in Oregon and Washington. The leaves, when rubbed, have the

strong odor characteristic of plants of the carrot family. The other striking feature of beach silver-top is the seasonal color change from the white flowers to the pinkish seed heads.

Caterpillars of the anise swallowtail and some cutworms feed on the leaves. Moon snail shells can be found under the seed heads of beach silver-top plants growing in the lower dunes. These predatory snails are widespread on sandy shores, where they search for bivalves in the wet sand.

Beach Silver-Top Community	
Herbivores	Predators
Anise swallowtail	Moon snail
Cutworm	

BEACH SILVER-TOP
(*Glehnia littoralis*: Apiaceae)
Characteristics: Long-taprooted perennial with shiny, compound, toothed basal leaves and clusters of whitish flowers borne at the tips of short leafless stalks. The seed heads become pinkish. The entire plant is closely appressed to the ground.
Habitat and range: Dunes from Alaska to northern California.
Comments: Beach silver-top often occurs in association with beach strawberry and beach morning glory.

ANISE SWALLOWTAIL

(*Papilio zelicaon*: Lepidoptera: Papilionidae)

Characteristics: The large mature caterpillars are quite striking, with alternating black and white rings on their body segments and most black rings containing yellow spots. The forked orange gland (osmeterium) in the neck emits a foul odor when extruded in defense.

Habitat and Range: Various habitats in western North America.

Comments: The caterpillars of this butterfly also develop on seacoast angelica as well as other plants in the carrot family.

CUTWORM

(Lepidoptera: Noctuidae)

Characteristics: Midsized orange-brown caterpillar with a light dorsal longitudinal band and a brown head capsule.

Habitat and range: Found only on beach silver-top in California.

Comments: The caterpillars feed on the leaves. Since the adult moth was not obtained, it is not known whether this is a generalist feeder or a specialist on beach silver-top.

MOON SNAIL

(*Pollinices lewisii*: Gastropoda: Naticidae)

Characteristics: Large snail with a wide shell opening to accommodate the large foot. Shell colors are white, blue, and brown.

Habitat and range: Widespread along the Pacific coast from Vancouver to Baja California.

Comments: These predaceous snails attack other mollusks. On some beaches their shells are often found under the leaves of beach silver-top. Moon snail eggs are deposited in a flattened, semicircular sandy case called a "sand collar."

SEASIDE PLANTAIN

Seaside plantain is a tenacious plant and, aside from growing on sand dunes, survives quite well on steep rock faces close to the ocean. In some locations it is joined by a recent introduction, the lobe-leaved seaside plantain. Their flowers are wind pollinated.

The slender leaves of seaside plantain don't provide much protection, so I searched for root-feeding insects. One herbivore in this microhabitat is a darkling beetle. The root-feeding lar- vae of these beetles are very slender, and it is difficult to imagine that they can trans- form into the robust brown adults that nibble on the leaves. The darkling beetles share this plant with greasy cutworm caterpillars that feed on the roots during the day and on the leaves at night.

A few additional insects choose to browse in the slender flower clusters. Small, inconspicuous green aphids and minute white scale insects suck juices from the flowers, and tan caterpillars feed among the seeds. While seaside plantain can be found growing on sand, the concentration of plants on rock ledges that contain roosting seabirds suggests that it utilizes guano as a source of nutrients.

SEASIDE PLANTAIN COMMUNITY
Herbivores
Darkling beetle
Greasy cutworm
Green plantain aphid
Plantain scale
Seed-head caterpillar

SEASIDE PLANTAIN

(*Plantago maritima*: Plantaginaceae)

Characteristics: Perennial with basal, linear, leathery, stemless leaves. Flowers inconspicuous, green, borne in dense spikes at the tips of erect leafless stalks. Fruit a capsule containing two to four brown seeds.

Habitat and range: Rocky cliffs and sand dunes along the Pacific Northwest coast. Seaside plantain also occurs in Europe, Africa, Asia, and South America.

Comments: An introduced European plant with similar habits is lobe-leaved seaside plantain (*Plantago coronopus*), with deeply incised leaves. Both species often occur in the same habitat and flower in the spring.

DARKLING BEETLE

(*Coniontis* sp.: Coleoptera: Tenebrionidae)

Characteristics: Larva midsized, long and slender, with cream-colored body and brown pronotum and head. Adult beetle midsized, shiny, brown, with irregular surface on wing covers (elytra) but smooth pronotum and head.

Habitat and range: Dunes in Oregon and California.

Comments: The larvae feed on the roots and the adults eat the leaves of seaside plantain. Other members of this beetle genus are pests of tomatoes, lima beans, and sugar beets.

GREASY CUTWORM
(*Agrotis ipsilon*: Lepidoptera: Noctuidae)
Characteristics: Smooth, shiny, midsized, brownish-gray caterpillar with dark bands running along the sides of the body. Adult moth has brown forewings with a pale area near the tip.
Habitat and range: Widespread throughout North America.
Comments: These caterpillars are generalist feeders. They eat the leaves of seaside plantain at night and hide in debris during the day.

GREEN PLANTAIN APHID
(Hemiptera: Aphididae)
Characteristics: A small, pale green aphid with short cornicles and reddish-brown eyes.
Habitat and range: Found only in Oregon on plants growing on rocky ledges.
Comments: These small aphids nestle among the flowers. No aphids have previously been reported from seaside plantain in North America.

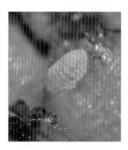

PLANTAIN SCALE
(Hemiptera: Coccidae)
Characteristics: A small, oval insect covered with powdery white scales. The legs are minute and hidden beneath the body.
Habitat and range: Found only in Oregon on seaside plantain.
Comments: These small insects feed on the developing seeds.

SEED-HEAD CATERPILLAR
(Lepidoptera)
Characteristics: A small tan caterpillar with a black head and pronotum and three faint broken yellow lines extending the length of the body. Each body segment bears minute dark spots.
Habitat and range: Rocky ledges and dunes in Oregon and California.
Comments: The caterpillars feed on the developing seeds. Adults were not obtained.

BEACH BUR

Well adapted to flat, exposed, sandy beaches, beach bur appears all along the Pacific coast. One interesting aspect of beach bur is the variation in leaf shape. Some plants have deeply lobed leaves, others have just slightly irregular margins, and still others show a range of intermediate forms between these two leaf shapes. The male and female flowers are separated on the flower stalks, with the green male flowers on the top and the dark female flowers below.

Insects have partitioned out beach bur, beginning at the top where little white maggots and their brown puparia are embedded in the flower clusters. Sharing the same habitat are picture-wing flies with strikingly patterned wings, which they slowly open and close when resting on the plants.

Farther down in the flower clusters are red-striped plume moth caterpillars that prefer to remain unseen. The adults are slender, gangly moths with long legs. The developing seeds serve as home for seed weevils. In preparing to oviposit, the small gray female seed weevil first makes a hole in the seedpod with her long snout, then turns around and deposits an egg deep inside it, and finally covers the entrance with plant or fecal material. After hatching, the weevil larva devours the seed and forms a pupa within the empty cavity.

Moving down the plant, we come to a rather nondescript white caterpillar that mines the leaves. One would never imagine that the moths they become are so brilliantly colored, which explains their name, jewel moth.

On beach bur stems are fuzzy galls, which are initiated when a female fly deposits her egg in the stem. The color, shape, and size of a gall are often specific to the particular insect that makes it. The round, greenish-brown gall covered with a thick layer of long whitish hairs identifies the maker as a small gnat of the family Cecidomyiidae, which contains numerous gall makers, all creating unique sculptures from living plant tissue. The gall not only provides protection for the developing maggot, but also supplies enough nutrients to carry the developing stages to maturity.

Inside the thick stems of beach bur is a white caterpillar that never leaves its feeding tunnel. When the adult moth emerges, its drab gray colors provide camouflage against the background of the drying stems. Some insect colors stand out and allow the bearer to be instantly recognized. These insects are usually bitter tasting, and the bright colors warn potential predators to keep away. An example on beach bur is the Asian spotted ladybird beetle, whose bright orange-red color and black spots immediately identify it. However, its chemical defenses make it unpalatable to many predators. These ladybird beetles come to dine on aphids or plant lice that suck sap from the stems of beach bur. Aphids have their own active defenses. A pair of slender, cannon-like structures (cornicles) on their backs are capable of discharging both defensive and alarm chemicals. These chemical weapons are not always successful, and I noticed some aphids using their back legs to kick at parasitic wasps. A better method is to receive aid from ants, and that can be achieved if the aphids produce attractive honeydew. When an ant is thirsty, it can stroke the back of an aphid with its antenna to bring forth a drop of honeydew. The ants are ready to attack any predators that enter the aphid's territory. Unfortunately, there were no ants protecting the beach bur aphids, and the brightly colored Asian ladybird beetles were able to satiate themselves.

Some generalist feeders, such as the caterpillars of the cabbage looper, locate beach bur far out in the dunes. Cabbage looper caterpillars are able to develop on a wide range of different plants (polyphagous), in contrast to specialized dune insects that feed on only a single plant species (monophagous).

BEACH BUR COMMUNITY	
Herbivores	Predators
Flower fly	Asian spotted ladybird beetle
Picture-wing fly	
Plume moth	
Seed weevil	
Fuzzy gall fly	
Stem moth	
Jewel moth	
Beach bur aphid	
Cabbage looper	

BEACH BUR
(*Ambrosia chamissonis*: Asteraceae)

Characteristics: A spreading perennial with prostrate stems bearing erect flower spikes. Leaves are covered with a layer of silvery hairs and vary in shape from deeply lobed to slightly notched. The tall, straight flowering spikes have greenish male flowers at the top and dark female flowers below. The flowering period is from July to September.

Habitat and range: Along the dunes from British Columbia to California.

Comments: The different leaf shape is notable. The ratio of the flower spike occupied by male and female flowers can be quite variable.

FLOWER FLY

(*Euarestoides acutangulus*: Diptera: Tephritidae)

Characteristics: Larvae small, roundish, grub-like, with black mouth hooks; puparia dark brown, ovate. Adult flies small, brownish gray, with large dark eyes and translucent wings with gray markings.

Habitat and range: Dunes from Washington to California.

Comments: The larvae feed on pollen in the unopened male flowers, and the pupae are formed in the flower heads.

PICTURE-WING FLY

(*Euaresta stelligera*: Diptera: Tephritidae)

Characteristics: A small fly with a relatively large head and eyes. Wings black with clear areas, especially along the borders. Larvae grub-like, white.

Habitat and range: Coastal areas from Canada to Baja California.

Comments: Picture-wing fly larvae occur in the same flower clusters as the larvae of flower flies but are larger and not as common.

PLUME MOTH

(*Adaina ambrosiae*: Lepidoptera: Pterophoridae)

Characteristics: Caterpillars midsized, with three to five deep reddish bands extending the length of the body. Pupae are elongated and light brown. Adult moths are midsized and slender, with long, narrow brown forewings and long legs.

Habitat and range: Dunes along the Pacific Northwest coast.

Comments: The caterpillars are deeply embedded within the flower heads and rarely emerge.

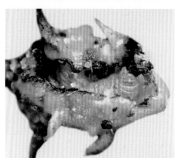

SEED WEEVIL

(*Apion* sp.: Coleoptera: Brentidae)

Characteristics: Larvae are small, white, curved, and legless. Adults are small, black, and pear shaped, with a small head and a long, curved beak.

Habitat and range: Dunes in California.

Comments: Larvae feed on seeds inside the female flowers. Adults visit flower spikes, especially during the evening.

FUZZY GALL FLY

(*Asphondylia ambrosiae*: Diptera: Cecidomyiidae)

Characteristics: Midsized round gall covered with a layer of long white plant hairs. The fly larva is small and white, with black mouth hooks.

Habitat and range: Dunes along the entire Pacific coast, especially in southern California.

Comments: The fly larvae feed on the gall tissue.

STEM MOTH
(*Epiblema* sp.: Lepidoptera: Olethreutidae)
Characteristics: Caterpillar midsized, white, with large, oval, dark head; pupa greenish yellow; adult moth midsized, uniformly light grayish brown.
Habitat and range: Dunes in California.
Comments: The caterpillars feed inside the stems of beach bur.

JEWEL MOTH
(*Caloreas* sp.: Lepidoptera: Choreutidae)
Characteristics: Caterpillar small and white, with a tan head and a spattering of minute brown spots over the body. The pale brown pupa is formed within a thick cocoon on the leaf surface. Adult moth is small but quite colorful, with the base of the forewing white and the remainder with various shades of brown, tan, white, and black.
Habitat and range: Found only along the Oregon coast.
Comments: The caterpillars of this moth appear late in the summer, and their activities cause the edges of the leaves to curl up, resulting in a shelter that is reinforced by webbing.

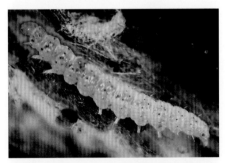

BEACH BUR APHID

(*Uroleucon ambrosiae*: Hemiptera: Aphididae)

Characteristics: Small brownish-gray aphids with extended cornicles, and antennae almost as long as the body.

Habitat and range: Dunes in California and elsewhere.

Comments: This aphid is attacked by Asian spotted ladybird beetles.

ASIAN SPOTTED LADYBIRD BEETLE

(*Harmonia axyridis*: Coleoptera: Coccinellidae)

Characteristics: Small beetle with orange to red wing covers (elytra) with black spots, and a black and white thorax. Young beetles often lack spots. Larvae dark brown, with broken red bands along sides of abdomen.

Habitat and range: Widespread throughout the United States.

Comments: This widespread beetle was introduced into North America from Japan for aphid control.

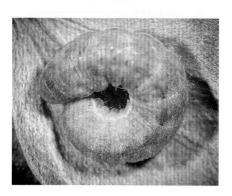

CABBAGE LOOPER

(*Trichoplusia ni*: Lepidoptera: Noctuidae)

Characteristics: Mature caterpillar midsized, robust, various shades of green. Adult moth brown, with mottled forewings bearing central white circular designs, and brown hind wings with white borders.

Habitat and range: Found only on beach bur in California dunes, but widespread throughout North America.

Comments: Cabbage looper has a wide host range, including cabbage and other vegetable crops.

DUNE PLANT COMMUNITIES: BEACH BUR

BEACH LAYIA

Beach layia is now found in only a few isolated dune systems in California. The horizontal orientation of many flowers during the blooming period from April to July is a curious feature of these endangered plants. While it was difficult for me to locate beach layia plants, spittlebugs were successful in finding isolated populations. These bugs are able to suck up plant juice and then expel it as frothy bubbles over themselves. Spittlebug feeding could stunt small plants such as beach layia or transmit viral pathogens.

Under some of the basal leaves of beach layia occur large, black, dune stink beetles. These beetles move slowly like armored vehicles across the dune sands, often completely exposing themselves to the midday sun. One would think their body temperature must rise to the boiling point, but their thick body wall protects them well. These beetles are flightless, and their fused wing covers protect their abdomen. Another survival tactic is to emit offensive secretions when they are disturbed. I noticed that the large wood ants that continuously patrol the dunes will not bother these beetles as long as they are healthy, but as soon as a beetle is injured or dies, the ants will fall upon it, cut it into pieces, and carry the severed body parts back to their nests.

BEACH LAYIA COMMUNITY
Herbivores
Spittlebug
Dune stink beetle

BEACH LAYIA
(*Layia carnosa*: Asteraceae)
Characteristics: A small, fleshy annual with lower leaves lobed and upper leaves entire. Flowers vary from white to yellow. Single to multiple flowers per plant.
Habitat and range: Endemic to several dune localities along the California coast.
Comments: This rare plant flowers from March to July and is on the federal endangered species list.

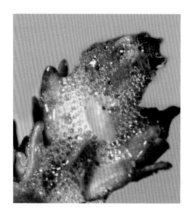

SPITTLEBUG

(Hemiptera: Cercopidae)

Characteristics: Immature bugs are small and yellowish and live within a mass of spittle. Adults are brown and winged.

Habitat and range: Dunes in California.

Comments: Since the host is endangered, any herbivorous insects are important. Spittlebugs not only weaken the plant by removing nutrients but can also transmit plant pathogens.

DUNE STINK BEETLE

(*Eleodes* sp.: Coleoptera: Tenebrionidae)

Characteristics: Large black beetle with thick body wall (cuticle), short antennae, and fairly long legs.

Habitat and range: Sand dunes from Washington to California.

Comments: These beetles are slow moving and both diurnal and nocturnal. They depend on their thick body armor and offensive chemicals for protection against predators. The larvae feed on roots of dune plants. Adults often occur under the basal leaves of beach layia.

YELLOW SAND VERBENA

Yellow sand verbena grows along the entire Pacific Coast. The round, bright yellow flower heads of this perennial stand out starkly against the dark green foliage. Whether bumblebees are attracted by the fragrance or bright color is unknown, but they frequently visit the blooms. In winter, the entire plant may disappear, but it reappears every spring with new leaves, drawing energy from reserves stored in the thick taproot that extends far down into the sand.

The undersurfaces of the thick green leaves are sticky from secretions released by stalked glands, and there are usually sand grains and the remains of unwary insects attached. The small, brown, nocturnal sand dune weevils must find the leaves repugnant, since they usually consume only the flowers. Freshly eaten leaves and adjacent prints in the sand show that rabbits dine on the leaves. Sand dune caterpillars have no trouble eating the top surface of the leaves but usually avoid the sticky undersides.

Caterpillars of the rare sand verbena spotted moth have an interesting feeding strategy. They lay their eggs on a leaf, and the hatchlings immediately burrow into it and start to eat the soft inner tissues in this protected habitat. When they have outgrown this niche, they initiate phase two. Now patterned with light and dark spots, a perfect camouflage that matches the color of sand grains, the caterpillars burrow in the sand during the day and come out at night to consume the leaves. The adult moths that emerge from the brown pupal cases have striped brown forewings that blend against the sandy background. As with so many insects, survival depends on concealment and camouflage.

Other caterpillars, like those of the tortricid and yellow woolly bear, feed throughout the day completely exposed on the leaves of yellow sand verbena. For protection, the tortricid spins a silken web over itself as it dines, and the yellow woolly bears are covered with stiff body hairs to keep their enemies at bay. The yellow woolly bear caterpillars ultimately metamorphose into beautiful white moths that fly at night.

A fluffy white mealybug eats in the leaf axils. Its body is dusted with slender white scales that easily detach, and spiders attempting to grasp these mealybugs may get only a pile of dried scales.

When the seedpods of yellow sand verbena are maturing, colorful milkweed bugs arrive to gorge themselves on the fruits. I suspect the flashy colors on the backs of these bugs are a warning that they taste bad. Brown sand dune beetles nibble on the roots of yellow sand verbena. While the adult beetles have an oval shape, the larvae are wormlike. These beetles are widespread throughout the dunes, where the larvae snack on plant roots. Also feeding on the roots of yellow sand verbena are cyst nematodes. As they mature, the slender females become swollen, cyst-like receptacles. These grape-shaped cysts are barely visible to the naked eye and have a hard covering that protects the developing eggs.

The beautiful Indian paintbrush gives no indication of its parasitic nature. However, the red foliage and apparent absence of chlorophyll are a hint that this plant does not produce its own food but takes nourishment from the roots of yellow sand verbena. While Indian paintbrush is doing what it must to survive, its striking red foliage and beautiful flowers mask its ominous underground behavior.

YELLOW SAND VERBENA COMMUNITY		
Herbivores	Predators	Parasites
Bumblebee	Spiders	Rove beetle nematode
Sand dune weevil	Dwarf rove beetle	Indian paintbrush
Brush rabbit		
Sand dune moth		
Spotted moth		
Tortricid caterpillar		
Yellow woolly bear moth		
Fluffy mealybug		
Small milkweed bug		
Dwarf rove beetle		
Thrip		
Cyst nematode		

YELLOW SAND VERBENA
(*Abronia latifolia*: Nyctaginaceae)
Characteristics: Perennial with deep taproot and fleshy, roundish, dark green leaves. Upper leaf surface smooth, lower leaf surface bearing many sticky, stalked glands. Flower clusters yellow, four- to five-lobed. Seedpods (fruits) fleshy, two- to three-angled.
Habitat and range: Along the Pacific coast from Washington to California.
Comments: Small insects are often found attached to the sticky leaves. Fragrance from the flowers that bloom during the summer is best detected during calm evenings.

SAND DUNE WEEVIL

(*Trigonoscuta* sp.: Coleoptera: Curculionidae)

Characteristics: Small, grayish-brown, short-snouted weevil with small dark eyes and short antennae.

Habitat and range: Sand dune weevils occur along the entire Pacific Northwest coast.

Comments: Adult weevils are especially fond of the flowers. The larvae develop on the roots.

BRUSH RABBIT

(*Sylvilagus bachmani*: Leporidae)

Characteristics: Grayish-brown rabbit with large dark eyes, relatively short ears, and a very short, cottony tail.

Habitat and range: Widespread along the entire Pacific Northwest coast and inland.

Comments: These rabbits rarely make burrows and usually hide under dense vegetation. Feeding is often restricted to early mornings. In some areas, they make pathways or short runways between adjacent yellow sand verbena plants.

SAND DUNE MOTH

(*Euxoa wilsoni*: Lepidoptera: Noctuidae)

Characteristics: Caterpillars midsized, with varying shades of brown, gray, and green that match the color of the sand. Body often with rows of light and dark interrupted bands. The end of the body is somewhat pointed. Adult moths large, with reddish-brown forewings ornamented with lighter markings.

Habitat and range: Dunes from British Columbia to California.

Comments: This genus occurs worldwide, with numerous species in the Pacific Northwest. The adult moths visit the flowers at night.

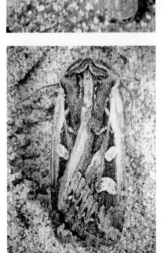

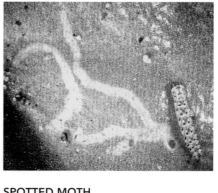

SPOTTED MOTH

(*Euphyia implicata*: Lepidoptera: Geometridae)

Characteristics: Caterpillars gray, covered with white, green, and black spots that mimic sand grains. Adult moths large, with forewings and abdomen marked by a series of light and dark bands.

Habitat and range: Dunes in California.

Comments: The eggs are deposited on the leaf surface, and the newly hatched caterpillars burrow into the leaf and initially feed as leaf miners. After reaching a certain size, they exit the leaves and reside in the sand during the day, coming out at night to dine on the foliage.

TORTRICID CATERPILLAR

(Lepidoptera: Tortricidae)

Characteristics: Caterpillar midsized, with a yellowish-green body and brown head.

Habitat and range: Found only on Oregon dunes.

Comments: The caterpillars feed under a loose protective web they spin on the leaf, leaving small holes in the leaf surface.

YELLOW WOOLLY BEAR MOTH

(Spilosoma virginica: Lepidoptera: Arctiidae)

Characteristics: Caterpillar large, with body bearing numerous clusters of long, stiff, white to yellow hairs, and narrow tufts of black hair at each end. Adult moth large, mostly white, with some small black spots on the wings. All abdominal segments with a central dorsal black spot. Head and thorax covered with long, silky scales.

Habitat and range: Found in various habitats throughout western North America.

Comments: The moths are nocturnal.

FLUFFY MEALYBUG

(Puto echinatus: Hemiptera: Putoidae)

Characteristics: Small, oval-shaped mealybug covered with numerous white scales.

Habitat and range: Along the entire Pacific coast and inland.

Comments: Fluffy mealybugs usually occur in the leaf axils of yellow sand verbena.

SMALL MILKWEED BUG

(Lygaeus kalmii: Hemiptera: Lygaeidae)

Characteristics: Adults with a red band across the thorax, a red cross on the forewings, and black spots on the thorax and wing covers. Wing tips black, usually with a pair of white spots (sometimes the white spots are absent).

Habitat and range: Along the coast from Vancouver to Baja California, and elsewhere inland.

Comments: These bugs take nectar from flowers and feed on seedpods. They are omnivores and prey on smaller insects.

THRIP
(Thysanoptera)

Characteristics: Very small, slender insects possessing sucking mouthparts, usually two pairs of narrow wings, short antennae, and a bladder-like structure on the tip of each leg.

Habitat and range: Associated with yellow sand verbena along the coast.

Comments: Thrips occur in both dune and strand habitats, especially on the flowers of the plants growing there. Along the coast, thrips are attacked by a number of insect predators, including small rove beetles.

DWARF ROVE BEETLE
(*Tarphiota geniculata*: Coleoptera: Staphylinidae)

Characteristics: Very small (under 3 mm long), elongated beetle with short wing covers that expose the abdomen, and a narrow head with bead-like antennae.

Habitat and range: Strands and lower dunes along the Pacific coast.

Comments: Dwarf rove beetles are predators that rest under dried seaweed during the day and forage at night for microinvertebrates. However, the rove beetles are themselves attacked and sterilized by a nematode parasite.

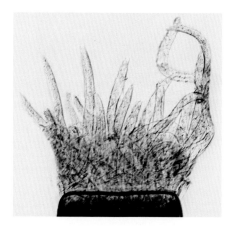

ROVE BEETLE NEMATODE
(*Proparasitylenchus californicus*: Tylenchida: Allantonematidae)

Characteristics: Mature females and juveniles inside infected beetles are worm-like, lacking segments and appendages and capable of only slow, sinuous movements.

Habitat and range: Thus far, found only in California, but could be widespread.

Comments: The infective-stage female nematode penetrates the larva of the dwarf rove beetle and develops into a mature female with eggs that hatch into juveniles inside the beetle's body cavity. The nematodes are carried into the adult beetle, where they mature, eventually killing the insect before emerging.

CYST NEMATODE

(*Heterodera* sp.: Nematoda: Heteroderidae)

Characteristics: Females minute, round, white when young, then maturing into brown, thick-walled cysts. Head region narrow, usually bent for feeding in root fissures. Mouth contains a minute feeding tube (stylet) that is inserted into plant cells for the uptake of plant juices.

Habitat and range: Cyst nematodes occur worldwide.

Comments: The thick body wall protects the eggs until they hatch. Cyst nematodes can retard plant growth when populations are high, and pathogenic fungi can invade the wounds they make.

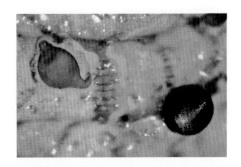

INDIAN PAINTBRUSH

(*Castilleja exserta*: Scrophulariaceae)

Characteristics: A parasitic annual with branching red stems and dissected red leaves. Flowers cream colored, overlapping, borne at the tips of the stems.

Habitat and range: Dunes in northern California.

Comments: The foliage of this Indian paintbrush root parasite of yellow sand verbena lacks any trace of green.

SEACOAST ANGELICA

Seacoast angelica is a keystone dune species and provides food for many herbivores. It can become quite large, with the flower head stalks reaching six feet tall or more. The wide, white flower clusters of seacoast angelica provide a good food source for an assortment of pollen- and nectar-feeding insects, including a variety of colorful longhorn beetles. A more dependable pollinator is the yellow-faced bumblebee, which often visits together with longhorn beetles and small sweat bees. Some bumblebees remain all night on the flowers, and I discovered that many of these are infected with a protozoan pathogen. Small yellowish caterpillars that feast on the maturing seeds of seacoast angelica are at times quite abundant. The rusty-colored adult moths fold their wings flat against their bodies, perhaps to reduce air friction, since the flower heads are continuously exposed to brisk coastal winds. Plump white maggots of the fancy fly develop in blotch leaf mines on seacoast angelica. When emerging from their puparia, the adult flies reveal beautiful iridescent eye colors.

The anise swallowtail butterfly lays dome-shaped eggs on the leaves of seacoast angelica, and the different developmental stages of the exposed caterpillars are unique. The young caterpillars are black except for their two middle segments, which are splashed with white and thus mimic a deposit of guano. Older caterpillars change their color pattern to light green with a series of black bands overlaid with yellow dots to better match the leaves of the host plant. If approached by a predator, they emit defensive compounds from an orange gland (osmeterium) extruded from the back of their neck.

But tachinid flies are still able to deposit their small white eggs on the caterpillars. Each egg is attached so tightly that it appears to have been glued with epoxy. At hatching, the maggots bore directly through the egg coating into the body cavity of the caterpillar, which eventually succumbs to the infection. Those caterpillars that finish their development construct a secure domicile or chrysalis that is attached to the plant by a thin but durable silk thread. The adults are beautiful black and yellow butterflies.

Using a different survival technique, the leaf moth caterpillar develops inside curled leaves or in the seed heads to avoid detection. The adults are unusual in having a row of scale tufts down the middle of their back.

Graceful two-spotted plant bugs normally feed on grass but occasionally switch to seacoast angelica. As they move over the stems, they may encounter colonies of spotted angelica aphids with rows of white markings on their backs.

SEACOAST ANGELICA COMMUNITY	
Herbivores	Parasites
Longhorn flower beetles	Bumblebee protozoan
Yellow-faced bumblebee	Tachinid fly
Sweat bee	
Seed-head caterpillar	
Fancy fly leaf miner	
Anise swallowtail	
Leaf moth	
Two-spotted plant bug	
Spotted angelica aphid	

SEACOAST ANGELICA

(*Angelica hendersonii*: Apiaceae)

Characteristics: Large, strong-scented, hollow-stemmed perennial with divided leaves. Leaflets irregularly toothed, green above, white woolly underneath. Flowers white, in numerous small heads arranged in flat-topped clusters (umbels) at the tips of branches. Fruits oblong, thick, with longitudinal ridges.

Habitat and range: Dunes and adjacent areas from Washington to California.

Comments: Seacoast angelica flowers during the summer and fall. It occurs only along the Pacific coast.

LONGHORN FLOWER BEETLES

(Coleoptera: Cerambycidae)

Characteristics: Midsized to large, elongated beetles with long antennae and legs. The thorax is usually narrower than the base of the wing covers. Two longhorn beetles commonly found on seacoast angelica are the parallel-sided longhorn (*Ortholeptura valida*) and the taper-sided longhorn (*Leptura obliterata*).

Habitat and range: Dune areas from Washington to California.

Comments: The larvae of longhorn beetles develop in dead wood, including trees that have burned in forest fires. They favor coniferous wood but also use hardwoods.

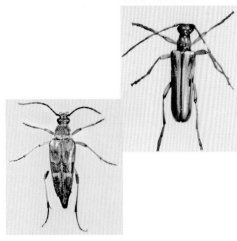

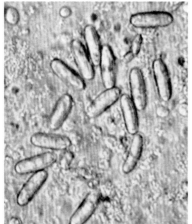

YELLOW-FACED BUMBLEBEE

(*Bombus vosnesenskii*: Hymenoptera: Apidae)

Characteristics: Large black bee with head, pronotum, and band around posterior portion of abdomen yellow.

Habitat and range: Throughout western North America.

Comments: This is one of the first bees to appear along the coast in the spring. Some individuals are parasitized by a protozoan pathogen (*Nosema* sp.: Nosematidae, left) that eventually kills them. Midsized sweat bees (Hymenoptera: Halictidae, top right), which are described elsewhere in this work, also visit the flowers.

SEED-HEAD CATERPILLAR

(*Agonopterix oregonensis*: Lepidoptera: Depressariidae)

Characteristics: Small, narrow, yellowish-green caterpillar with a black head and pronotum. Pupa reddish brown, robust. Adult moth midsized, with rusty-colored forewings rounded at the tips and held flat against the abdomen.

Habitat and range: Dunes from British Columbia to California.

Comments: The caterpillars can be quite numerous in flower heads and must reduce seed production.

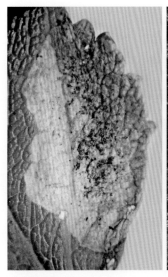

FANCY FLY

(Euleia fratria: Diptera: Tephritidae)

Characteristics: Larva small, maggot-like, yellowish white, with black mouth hooks and breathing pores (stigmata) at the posterior end. Puparium robust, yellow turning to brown, in flower heads. Adult fly small, reddish brown, with large iridescent eyes and grayish wings with light blotches.

Habitat and range: Dunes along the Pacific coast and elsewhere in North America.

Comments: While most of the larvae develop in blotch leaf mines, some also feed in the flower heads.

ANISE SWALLOWTAIL
(*Papilio zelicaon*: Lepidoptera: Papilionidae)

Characteristics: Eggs minute, white, hemispherical, ornamented on surface. Young caterpillars dark brown, with short spines and a white blotch in the middle of the back. Older caterpillars become large, lose their spines, and turn light green, with transverse black bands containing yellow spots on the body segments. When the caterpillar is disturbed, a forked orange gland (osmeterium) that emits defensive chemicals is extruded from the back of the neck. The large light green chrysalis is attached to the stem of the plant by a single thick strand of silk. The adults are very large and have yellow wings with black markings.

Habitat and range: Various habitats in western North America.

Comments: The blotchy markings on the young caterpillars mimic bird droppings. The osmeterium, which occurs only in mature caterpillars, emits a foul odor. Tiny white tachinid fly eggs (left center) deposited on the caterpillars hatch into maggots that bore into the victim and devour it from the inside.

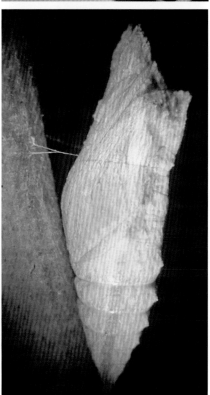

LEAF MOTH

(*Epermenia* sp.: Lepidoptera:
Epermeniidae)

Characteristics: Caterpillar small, cream
colored, with three faint brown bands
running the length of its body. Head and
pronotum dark brown. Pupa small, greenish brown, slender. Adult moth midsized,
brown, with a row of three scale tufts on
its back, with the anterior tuft largest and
the posterior smallest.

Habitat and range: Dunes in California
and Oregon.

Comments: The caterpillars reside
within curled leaves or occasionally in
the flower heads. The pupae occur in the
same location.

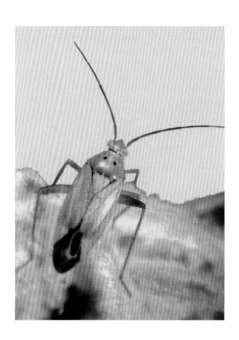

TWO-SPOTTED PLANT BUG

(*Stenotus binotatus*: Hemiptera: Miridae)

Characteristics: Small, slender, greenish-brown (there is considerable color variation) plant bug with light brown eyes, dark wing tips, and two minute dots on the prothorax.

Habitat and range: Originally from Europe, this bug is now widely distributed in North America.

Comments: This bug is a generalist feeder and an occasional visitor on seacoast angelica.

SPOTTED ANGELICA APHID

(*Aphis* sp.: Hemiptera: Aphididae)

Characteristics: Small grayish-green aphids with transverse rows of interrupted white bands on their abdomens.

Habitat and range: Dunes in Washington and Oregon.

Comments: These aphids feed on the flower stalks of seacoast angelica.

BEACH KNOTWEED

Like so many dune plants, beach knotweed has acquired characteristics that resist the strong coastal winds. The plants are small and have decumbent stems, rhizomes, and slender, thick, somewhat leathery leaves. Also, the leaf margins are so tightly inrolled that it is impossible to straighten them without tearing the leaf.

The pink to white flowers attract butterflies, including the mariposa copper, as well as flower scarab beetles. While the caterpillars of the mariposa copper butterfly feed on the leaves of beach knotweed, the grubs of the flower scarab develop on the roots of this and other dune plants. Flea beetle larvae and adults chew up the rounded margins of the leaves. The adult beetles are named appropriately since they can jump like fleas. The basal portion of their legs is swollen, and by crouching and then suddenly straightening out their legs, they are propelled several feet in the air. The jump happens so quickly that it is often impossible to see where the beetle lands.

By carefully peeling back some webbed leaves, you can often get a quick glimpse of the oblique-banded leaf-roller caterpillar before it wiggles back to the safety of its webbed domain. When a pupa is discovered among the rolled-up leaves, it will vibrate its abdomen, a behavior that may have survival value. The reddish-brown adult moths remain motionless when exposed and are well camouflaged against the plant stems.

In the spring, during the beginning of the flowering period, most beach knotweed plants have a few spittlebug nymphs on them, producing their protective layer of spittle. But it is the related armored scale insects that are the most fascinating. These insects have evolved a unique method of development. The female scale insect looks like a brown dome attached to the leaf, and her body is essentially covered by a waxy shell. She has no eyes, legs, antennae, or wings, and her body is essentially just digestive and reproductive systems with a beak. When she emerged from the egg, she had functional legs and could crawl around over the leaves. But as soon as she molted, she lost her power of locomotion and became both stationary and solitary. She doesn't produce honeydew like other types of scale insects, so there are no ants to accompany or protect her. But she still molts and grows, converting plant juices into wax that is used to enlarge her shell. Her sole duty now is reproduction. But such a unique life is not without its problems. Some scale insects are infected with a protozoan pathogen and die before they can produce any eggs or young.

BEACH KNOTWEED COMMUNITY	
Herbivores	Parasites
Mariposa copper butterfly	Protozoa
Flower scarab	
Sand dune wasp	
Flea beetle	
Spittlebug nymph	
Oblique-banded leaf roller	
Armored scale	

BEACH KNOTWEED

(*Polygonum paronychia*: Polygonaceae)
Characteristics: A low-growing, partially woody perennial with stems prostrate to erect. Leaves slender, stiff, shiny, margins inrolled, clustered at branch tips. Flowers small, white to pink, clustered in upper leaf axils.
Habitat and range: Dunes from British Columbia to California.
Comments: Beach knotweed has a large number of flower visitors in the spring, especially bees, but also butterflies and beetles.

MARIPOSA COPPER BUTTERFLY

(*Epidemia mariposa*: Lepidoptera: Lycaenidae)
Characteristics: Adult large, with brown-spotted orange wings with brown and white margins. Caterpillar sluglike, greenish brown.
Habitat and range: Dunes from British Columbia to California.
Comments: The caterpillars are well camouflaged as they feed on the leaves.

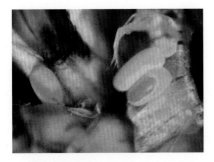

FLEA BEETLE

(*Altica* sp.: Coleoptera: Chrysomelidae)

Characteristics: Eggs elongated, cream colored when laid, darkening with age. Larvae small, gray black, covered with small, flat warts and short, erect hairs. Adults small, shiny coppery black.

Habitat and range: Dunes from Washington to California.

Comments: The eggs are deposited at the base of the leaves. The inconspicuous larvae are usually hidden within the leaf clusters.

FLOWER SCARAB

(*Serica* sp.: Coleoptera: Scarabaeidae)

Characteristics: Midsized, dull black beetle with a broad head and short, clubbed antennae. The whitish, C-shaped grubs develop on plant roots.

Habitat and range: Widespread along the Pacific coast as well as inland.

Comments: These beetles are good fliers and visit a variety of flowers for pollen and nectar. Sand dune wasps (*Bembix* sp.: Hymenoptera: Crabronidae), described elsewhere in this work, also visit the flowers for nectar.

SPITTLEBUG NYMPH

(Hemiptera: Cercopidae)

Characteristics: Small, pale yellow body with dark reddish-brown eyes and short, straight antennae.

Habitat and range: Widespread along the Pacific coast.

Comments: The nymphs live within a mass of "spittle."

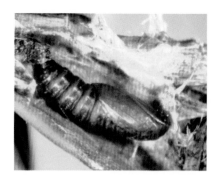

OBLIQUE-BANDED LEAF ROLLER
(*Choristoneura rosaceana*: Lepidoptera: Tortricidae)

Characteristics: Caterpillars are small and various shades of green, with a dark head. The pupae are brownish. The small adults are reddish brown, with a diffuse broad dark circle on the folded wings and dark bands along the tips of the forewings.
Habitat and range: Dunes from Washington to California.
Comments: The caterpillars hide among the basal leaves during the day, coming out at night to feed.

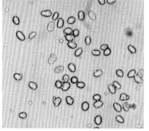

ARMORED SCALE
(Hemiptera: Diaspididae)

Characteristics: Small, tan, rigid, domed, smooth scale insect.
Habitat and range: Dunes in Oregon.
Comments: The dome is actually a waxy covering over the underlying insect, which sucks sap from the plant tissues. The pictured specimen was infected by a protozoan pathogen.

THRIFT

The clustered pink flowers of thrift in late spring and early summer are always a welcome sight, whether they are growing on the flat sandy dunes of Oregon or the sandy cliffs along the California coast. This versatile plant even grows on rock ledges near nesting seabirds. The tight clusters of narrow leaves hug the ground tightly, and the length of the flower stems is an indication of the wind velocity at that particular site. On exposed cliffs the flower stems barely rise above the surface, while lower down on the dunes they are much higher.

Thrift flowers appear to be one of the favorite visiting spots of the quick little acmon blue butterflies, so the nectar must be plentiful. Their striking blue color contrasts against the pink flowers. Other insects on the blooms are tiny soft-winged flower beetles that crawl over the petals or, more commonly, lie with their heads deeply inserted in the tubular flowers. Often only the tip of their abdomen is visible. Many are so preoccupied with imbibing the nectar that they don't even notice when the flowers are picked. Even when touched, they show little sign of irritation and just emerge from the blooms and crawl to some neighboring flowers.

Green caterpillars are hidden among the bracts, which furnish food as well as protection. Touching one of these causes it to wiggle backward and drop into the mass of slender leaves at the base of the flower stalks. Even more curious are the short brown caterpillars that feed on the dried flowers long after the blooms are gone. The white-crowned sparrows that come to feed on the seeds may include a few of these caterpillars as a side dish. White-crowned sparrows are one of the most common ground birds in the dune habitat and often build their nests in dune shrubs or in trees in the back dunes.

THRIFT COMMUNITY
Herbivores
Acmon blue butterfly
Soft-winged flower beetle
Flower-bract caterpillar
Dried-flower caterpillar
White-crowned sparrow

THRIFT, SEA-PINK

(*Armeria maritima*: Plumbaginaceae)

Characteristics: Small perennial with narrow, clustered basal leaves and rhizomes. Flowers are various shades of pink and bloom from April to July. The blooms are in tight clusters at the tips of leafless stalks.

Habitat and range: Dunes, beaches, and sandy cliffs from Canada to California.

Comments: Herbivores on this beautiful small plant are not common, and those that occur seem to prefer the flowers. White-crowned sparrows relish the seeds.

ACMON BLUE BUTTERFLY

(*Plebejus acmon*: Lepidoptera: Lycaenidae)

Characteristics: Midsized blue butterfly with a black and white border on the front wings and a red, black-dotted, solid black and white border on the hind wings.

Habitat and range: From Washington to California and elsewhere.

Comments: The caterpillars feed on coast buckwheat, trefoil, and lupines in the dune environment.

SOFT-WINGED FLOWER BEETLE

(*Enallonyx denudatus*: Coleoptera: Melyridae)

Characteristics: Small, elliptical, brown to black beetle with wide thorax and eleven-segmented, bead-like antennae. Body covered with appressed hairs.

Habitat and range: Dunes from Washington to California.

Comments: The adult beetles spend hours with their heads embedded in thrift flowers, feeding on pollen and nectar. The larvae are scavengers and feed on plant and animal remains in dune habitats.

FLOWER-BRACT CATERPILLAR
(Lepidoptera)
Characteristics: Small, pale green caterpillar bearing black spots on each body segment, and a black head.
Habitat and range: Dunes in Oregon.
Comments: The caterpillars bind the flower bracts together and feed inside them.

DRIED-FLOWER CATERPILLAR
(Lepidoptera)
Characteristics: Small, tan to brown caterpillar covered with stiff setae.
Habitat and range: Dunes in Oregon.
Comments: The caterpillars are buried deeply in dried flower clusters that have finished blooming, and they probably eat the seeds.

WHITE-CROWNED SPARROW
(*Zonotrichia leucophrys*)
Characteristics: A small sparrow with brown wings streaked with white, a gray breast, and black and white stripes on its head. The bill is yellow or pinkish.
Habitat and range: Year-round resident along most of the Pacific coast.
Comments: White-crowned sparrows are one of the most common small birds in the dunes and include thrift seeds in their diet. They make their nests under shrubs, bushes, or trees throughout the dunes.

COASTAL SAGEWORT

It is the woolly grayish-green foliage, tiny dissected leaves, and strong aroma that identify coastal sagewort. Because it has such small leaves and slender flower stalks, there are few areas for herbivores to hide. However, a small caterpillar still manages to bind leaves together with silk to make a hidden feeding enclosure.

Helfer's dune grasshopper isn't shy about feeding on the stems. You will usually first notice these grasshoppers taking flight as you approach the plant. The nymphs, with their black and orange bodies that mimic the hues of sand grains, are nearly invisible. Dune grasshoppers depend on camouflage or a quick jump followed by a short flight to escape their enemies. They are targeted by snakes, lizards, birds, and small mammals.

Jerusalem crickets depend on a different survival strategy. Although they are clearly visible against the sandy background, they remain in burrows or under wood and other debris during the day. They often feed on the roots of coastal sagewort from their burrows. They are wingless and can't jump or run fast, so a quick escape is out of the question. However, their large heads bear a powerful set of mandibles that can draw blood when handled. Nevertheless, deer mice will make a meal from Jerusalem crickets.

Another enemy of the Jerusalem cricket is a parasitic hairworm that grows to two to three times the length of its victim. To be successful, the mature parasite must undergo a complex behavior that begins by "guiding" its host to a water source. As the infected Jerusalem cricket enters the water, the hairworms emerge, mate, and deposit their eggs. Midge larvae that eat the eggs are the intermediate host. The parasites remain in the midges until they are eaten by an omnivorous Jerusalem cricket.

A very obvious insect predator is the northern alligator lizard. Moving up ever so slowly on its prey, the lizard judges just when it can lunge. While grasshoppers can still flee if they jump quickly enough, the Jerusalem cricket has little chance of escape. A large predator that will attack grasshoppers, Jerusalem crickets, and even lizards and snakes is the California ground squirrel. Ground squirrels are well known to serve as reservoir hosts to the plague organism, which is transmitted from one to another by fleas.

The red and yellow flowers of the seashore paintbrush are much more striking than the dull-colored flowers of coastal sagewort. However, their beauty is marred by the knowledge that seashore paintbrush parasitizes the roots of coastal sagewort. Coastal sagewort plants that die from various causes provide food for subterranean termites that inhabit the woody stems.

COASTAL SAGEWORT COMMUNITY		
Herbivores	Parasites	Predators
Leaf caterpillar	Hairworm	Northern alligator lizard
Helfer's dune grasshopper	Seashore paintbrush	Deer mouse
Jerusalem cricket		Western garter snake
Subterranean termites		California ground squirrel

COASTAL SAGEWORT

(*Artemisia pycnocephala*: Asteraceae)
Characteristics: Aromatic leafy perennial bearing small, dissected, woolly leaves along the stem. Flowers, which appear from July to September, are borne in clusters of small heads at the tips of the stems.
Habitat and range: Dunes in Oregon and California.
Comments: Few herbivores are found on coastal sagewort, perhaps because of its aromatic compounds.

LEAF CATERPILLAR

(*Phaneta* sp.: Lepidoptera: Tortricidae)
Characteristics: Small grayish-green caterpillar, with brown prothorax and head capsule.
Habitat and range: Dunes in California.
Comments: These caterpillars reside inside woven tubes constructed with leaf parts.

HELFER'S DUNE GRASSHOPPER

(*Trimerotropis helferi*: Orthoptera: Acrididae)

Characteristics: Adults large, brown, speckled with small dark and white spots that match the sand particles. Nymphs are yellowish brown and almost invisible when resting on sand.

Habitat and range: Dunes in Oregon and California.

Comments: This is a solitary species limited to areas along the Pacific coast. The color patterns on the body vary somewhat depending on the geographic location.

JERUSALEM CRICKET

(*Stenopelmatus* sp.: Orthoptera: Stenopelmatidae)

Characteristics: Large, brown, flightless, cricket-like insect with a smooth, shiny body, black-striped abdomen, wide head, and slender antennae. All legs are well developed, with the forelegs modified somewhat for digging.

Habitat and range: Found under wood and rocks and in burrows along the coast and inland throughout western North America.

Comments: These omnivorous insects are burrowers and tunnel under coastal sagewort to feed on the roots. The juveniles are similar in appearance to the adults. They make sounds by drumming their abdomen against the ground. Two of their predators are lizards and snakes, and they are parasitized by hairworms.

DUNE PLANT COMMUNITIES: COASTAL SAGEWORT

HAIRWORM

(*Neochordodes occidentalis*:
Nematomorpha: Chordodidae)
Characteristics: Long, narrow, black or
brown wormlike body lacking segments
and appendages.
Habitat and range: Found on dunes in
Oregon and California.
Comments: After leaving their hosts,
adult hairworms mate and the females
deposit their eggs in water. Upon hatching, the juveniles enter the body of an
aquatic insect but can develop further
only when that insect is ingested by a
Jerusalem cricket.

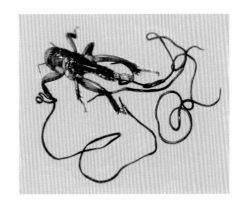

NORTHERN ALLIGATOR LIZARD

(*Elgaria coerulea*: Reptilia: Anguidae)
Characteristics: A large, gray to brown
lizard with short legs and a long tail. The
back often bears a row of dark blotches.
The scales on the back are separated from
those on the belly by a conspicuous skin
fold.
Habitat and range: Dunes and adjacent
portions of British Columbia, Washington,
Oregon, and northern California.
Comments: These lizards occur under
driftwood and vegetation in sand dunes.
Food consists of insects (including
Jerusalem crickets), spiders, and other
lizards.

WESTERN GARTER SNAKE

(*Thamnophis elegans*: Squamata:
Colubridae)
Characteristics: A slender brown snake
with a red or yellow middorsal line and a
yellow line on each side of the body.
Habitat and range: Along the Pacific
coast from Washington to California.
Comments: Color patterns can vary
considerably. When captured, they release
feces and offensive secretions from their
anal glands. Garter snakes are live bearing
and consume a wide range of invertebrates and small vertebrates.

CALIFORNIA GROUND SQUIRREL

(*Citellus beecheyi*: Rodentia: Sciuridae)

Characteristics: Body mostly brown with white flecks. Light region on the back of the neck extends backward, partially bordering a dark triangular region in the middle of the upper back. Tail brown, bushy.

Habitat and Range: Along the Pacific coast from Washington to California.

Comments: This is a diurnal species that raises its young in burrows. It is omnivorous and eats a range of animal prey, including grasshoppers, Jerusalem crickets, and even snakes and lizards. Unfortunately, it is a reservoir host for the plague organism (*Yersinia pestis*), which can be transmitted to humans through the bite of a flea.

SEASHORE PAINTBRUSH

(*Castilleja affinis*: Scrophulariaceae)

Characteristics: An erect, semiparasitic perennial with long, yellow, red-tipped flowers and oblong, usually entire, villous leaves. A fuzzy pubescence occurs on all parts of the plant, including the flowers. Stems arise from the base of the host plant.

Habitat and range: Coastal dunes and bluffs from Washington to Baja California.

Comments: Seashore paintbrush has suckers that obtain nutrients from the roots of other dune plants besides coastal sagewort, such as beach wormwood and coyote bush. Seashore paintbrush is pollinated by hummingbirds.

SAND DUNE PHACELIA

The deeply ribbed, silvery-green leaves quickly identify sand dune phacelia, a rare native plant found only on the coastal dunes of northern California and southern Oregon. As a result of the removal of dune habitats and the introduction of competitive exotic plants, sand dune phacelia is heading toward extinction. Nevertheless, the few remaining plants have some interesting associates, including pollinators like bumblebees and leaf-cutter bees (*Anthidium* sp.: Hymenoptera: Megachilidae), and leaf feeders such as sand dune weevils (*Trigonoscuta* sp.: Coleoptera: Curculionidae), scale insects (Hemiptera: Coccidae), stem-boring caterpillars (Lepidoptera: Hepialidae) that tunnel through the thick woody stems of older plants, and garden snails (*Helix aspersa*: Gastropoda: Helicidae).

SAND DUNE PHACELIA COMMUNITY
Herbivores
Bumblebee
Leaf-cutter bee
Leaf weevil
Spittlebug
Scale insects
Stem-boring caterpillars
Garden snail

SAND DUNE PHACELIA

(*Phacelia argentea*: Hydrophyllaceae)

Characteristics: Prostrate to ascending perennial with oval, deeply ribbed, silver-haired leaves and small, white to slightly pinkish flowers borne in terminal clusters.

Habitat and range: Dunes in Oregon and California.

Comments: Sand dune phacelia is a rare summer-blooming plant that appears to be on the verge of extinction.

BUMBLEBEE

(*Bombus* sp.: Hymenoptera: Apidae)

Characteristics: Small black bee with hairy head and thorax and white bars on the abdomen.

Habitat and range: Dunes from Washington to California.

Comments: Bumblebees are probably the main pollinators of sand dune phacelia.

SPITTLEBUG

(Hemiptera: Cercopidae)

Characteristics: Small, elliptical brown bug with a pointed snout and streamlined body. At rest, the wings are held vertically.

Habitat and range: Dunes in Oregon and California.

Comments: The immature stages develop within a mass of "spittle" that they produce from plant juices.

SEASHORE LUPINE

If any dune plant is a keystone species, it is seashore lupine. That this small plant has managed to survive along with marram grass is fortunate for all the organisms that depend on it. One of these is an attractive leaf beetle. The larvae are covered with small bumps and short hairs and stand out against the green leaves. The pupae, which are found in the sand, change from light brown to almost black as they mature. The adults are similar in color to the larvae and, after a period of rapid feeding, turn their activities to mating and egg laying. These leaf beetles are sometimes quite numerous, and it is not uncommon to see scores of larvae on a single plant, sometimes even denuding it. The area around seashore lupine is often occupied by dune ants that are effective predators. The worker ants rush at beetles that have fallen to the sand but, after inspecting them, back away. The beetles have clearly devised some method of repelling the ants.

In contrast to the leaf beetles, the stem weevil is solitary and will tolerate another of its species only when mating. Both the adults and larvae characteristically develop inside the stems of seashore lupine.

Curiously, some leaflets of seashore lupine are not flat like the others but are roundish and look like red-tipped fingers. This malformation is initiated by a small fly that introduces a stimulant into the leaves along with its eggs. It causes the leaves to swell and their edges to roll inward, thus providing an enclosed protective habitat for the small yellow fly maggots.

One of the most interesting insects on seaside lupine is a slender caterpillar that constructs long silken tubes under or on the surface of the sand. These, which can extend almost a foot in length, are camouflaged with attached sand grains. Pulling them apart is impossible; the silk is woven so tightly that it can be cut open only with a small pair of scissors. The light green caterpillars inside move with a kind of loping motion. When freed, the caterpillars quickly scurry out of reach. The slender light green pupae hidden in the sand are very sensitive and immediately vibrate when disturbed. The adult moths run and hop over the sand. They are not willing to fly even though they appear to have well-developed wings. Perhaps they fear the strong coastal winds that could blow them quite a distance from their egg-laying sites.

Leaf stalks that are tightly curled and twisted are a sign of infection by the petiole curl fungus. Trying to straighten these stalks is futile since they break easily. The inner tissues are filled with cells of a microscopic fungus that produces spores on the stalk's surface. In some areas, seashore lupine is attacked by a parasitic plant known as dodder, a yellow vine that produces small protuberances on its stems. As it coils around seaside lupine, the protuberances penetrate the tissues of its victim. After obtaining nourishment from seashore lupine, dodder forms innocent-looking white flowers.

Also infecting the roots of seashore lupine is the fungal mycelium of the lackluster mushroom. However, this is a symbiotic mycorrhizal association that benefits both organisms. Evidence of nitrogen-fixing bacteria is obvious from the presence of swollen lumps or nodules on the roots of seaside lupine. These are where microorganisms convert nitrogen in the atmosphere to nitrogenous growth compounds the plant can use.

SEASHORE LUPINE COMMUNITY		
Herbivores	Symbionts	Parasites
Leaf beetle	Nitrogen-fixing bacteria	Dodder
Stem weevil	Lackluster mushroom	Petiole curl fungus
Leaf gall fly		
Sand tube moth		
Pod moth		
Stem fly		
Painted lady butterfly		
Rusty moth		
Brown sand caterpillar		
Green sand caterpillar		

SEASHORE LUPINE
(*Lupinus littoralis*: Fabaceae)
Characteristics: Much-branched perennial with trailing stems, sometimes forming mats. Leaves palmately compound with six to eight leaflets. Pealike blue flowers borne in clusters. Pods hairy, with pealike seeds.
Habitat and range: Dunes from British Columbia to California.
Comments: Seashore lupine grows in a number of dune habitats and is host to a variety of organisms.

LEAF BEETLE

(*Galeruca rudis*: Coleoptera: Chrysomelidae)

Characteristics: Larva tan when young, darkening to black when older, covered with small protrusions bearing hairs. Pupa tan, gradually darkening. Adult small, black, with striated wing covers with orange to yellow margins.

Habitat and range: Dunes in Oregon and California.

Comments: Large numbers can denude the plants. Most larvae scrape away the surface of the leaves, leaving behind a trail of their feeding activity. Common dune ants (*Formica* sp.: Hymenoptera: Formicidae) show no interest in these beetles.

STEM WEEVIL

(*Lixus* sp.: Coleoptera: Curculionidae)

Characteristics: Midsized, elongated brown weevil with a tan abdomen and a stout, slightly curved beak. Larvae white, legless, with a black head.

Habitat and range: Dunes in Oregon and California.

Comments: The eggs are deposited in the stems, which the larvae mine. The adults feed on the foliage and hibernate within the stems.

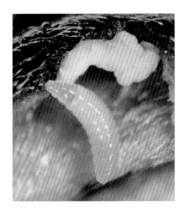

LEAF GALL FLY
(*Dasineura lupini*: Diptera: Cecidomyiidae)
Characteristics: Larvae small, cream to yellow. Adult flies dark, with long legs and antennae.
Habitat and range: Dunes in California.
Comments: The larvae occur within the swollen leaflet galls, which turn reddish toward the tips.

SAND TUBE MOTH
(*Areniscythris* sp.: Lepidoptera: Scythrididae)
Characteristics: Caterpillar elongated, with small legs, uniformly pale to greenish, sometime with faint red longitudinal lines. Pupa slender, greenish. Adult moth small, with long antennae and brown wings with black and white patches.
Habitat and range: Dunes in Oregon and California.
Comments: The caterpillars build and live in long silken tubes that are attached to the stems and extend some distance under the sand. The adults have wings but, instead of flying, have a type of hopping-running behavior.

POD MOTH

(*Chionodes* sp.: Lepidoptera: Gelechiidae)

Characteristics: Caterpillars gray, with brown head and pronotum. Moths small, with long antennae and brown mottling on forewings.

Habitat and range: Dunes in Oregon and California.

Comments: The larvae feed on the developing pods of seashore lupine.

STEM FLY

(*Delia lupini*: Diptera: Anthomyiidae)

Characteristics: Larva maggot-like, white with black mouth hooks. Adult small, brownish gray, with transparent wings and large eyes.

Habitat and range: Dunes from Washington to California.

Comments: The larvae and puparia occur in the stems.

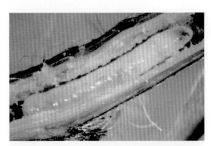

PAINTED LADY BUTTERFLY
(*Vanessa cardui*: Lepidoptera: Nymphalidae)

Characteristics: Caterpillar black, body covered with fine white specks, a few yellow blotches, and bristly spines. Adult very large, with black and orange forewings with white blotches. Hind wings are orange with a series of black spots and dashes.

Habitat and range: Widespread throughout the Pacific coastal region.

Comments: This butterfly is very common in the Pacific Northwest. The caterpillars can develop on a range of plants, but apparently only those on seashore lupine have yellow spots.

RUSTY MOTH
(*Staudingeria albipennella*: Lepidoptera: Pyralidae)

Characteristics: Caterpillar pale below but brownish green above, with black dots. Head tan with a few darker spots. Adult moth small, slender, with reddish-brown wings with some gray areas.

Habitat and range: Dunes in Oregon and California.

Comments: The caterpillars feed on the leaves of seaside lupine.

BROWN SAND CATERPILLAR

(*Lasionycta* sp.: Lepidoptera: Noctuidae)

Characteristics: Caterpillar light brown, with two longitudinal lines on the back, dark spiracles, and a tan head with a few brown spots. Adult moth large, with gray forewings intersected with irregular black diamond-shaped markings.

Habitat and range: Dunes in Oregon and California.

Comments: The caterpillars, which are rapid diggers, remain in the sand during the day and feed at night.

GREEN SAND CATERPILLAR

(*Dryotype opina*: Lepidoptera: Noctuidae)

Characteristics: Caterpillar bright green, with white spiracles and a green head. Adult moth large, brown, with a dark spot and two curved dark lines on the underside of the hind wings.

Habitat and range: Dunes from Washington to California.

Comments: The bright green caterpillars are quite striking and feed aboveground only at night, remaining in the sand during the day.

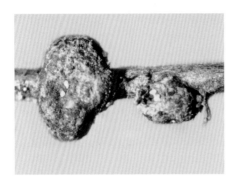

NITROGEN-FIXING BACTERIA
(*Rhizobium lupini*: Rhizobiales: Rhizobiaceae)

Characteristics: *Rhizobium* bacteria are motile, non-spore-forming rods. They live in ovoid to round nodules that are firmly attached to or encircle the root and appear as galls.

Habitat and range: Throughout the dune area from Washington to California.

Comments: *Rhizobium* nodules are where biological nitrogen fixation occurs. This is an obligate association, with both organisms dependent on the other for survival.

DODDER
(*Cuscuta* sp.: Cuscutaceae)

Characteristics: Dodder is a highly modified flowering plant that has lost its chlorophyll as a result of parasitism. The yellowish stems are vine-like and have minute scale-like leaves. The stems have small protuberances or suckers that attach to and penetrate seaside lupine. The petals of the small white flowers with yellow anthers are fused.

Habitat and range: Throughout the Pacific Northwest on various plants.

Comments: The seeds germinate into short stems that make contact with seaside lupine. After twining around its victim, dodder forms protrusions that penetrate the host for moisture and nutrients. Once established, dodder severs contact with the soil and becomes completely parasitic. There are many species and varieties of dodder, which can be identified by their physical characteristics and host plants.

PETIOLE CURL FUNGUS

(Fungi: Chytridiomycetes)

Characteristics: This fungus lives inside the petioles of seashore lupine and causes them to become S-shaped. The surface of the infected petioles contains groups (sori) of developing spores.

Habitat and range: Dunes in Oregon.

Comments: Aside from the twisted petioles, there are no additional signs of the infection.

LACKLUSTER MUSHROOM

(*Laccaria laccata*: Agaricales: Hydnangiaceae)

Characteristics: Small to medium-sized, brown to tan mushroom with a centrally depressed cap, flesh-colored attached gills, and white spores.

Habitat and range: Widespread in sand dunes, dune forests, and other sandy habitats.

Comments: This mushroom forms a mycorrhizal association with seashore lupine that benefits both organisms.

MINER'S LETTUCE

MINER'S LETTUCE

(*Claytonia rubra* subsp. *depressa*: Portulacaceae)

Characteristics: Small, succulent, glabrous annual that forms circular mats in the sand. The basal leaves are broadly heart shaped with truncate bases. The stem leaves, which serve as receptacles for clusters of small white flowers, can be almost circular. Flowering occurs from February to June.

Habitat and range: Dunes from Washington to California and elsewhere.

Comments: Miner's lettuce received its name in reference to its use as a leaf vegetable by miners, especially those of the California Gold Rush. Another common annual species of *Claytonia* growing on sand dunes is pale claytonia (*Claytonia exigua*), with narrow leaves and white to pink flowers. Pale claytonia is self-fertilized, which explains why the flowers do not attract pollinators.

SAND MAT

If there is a dune plant I hesitate to examine, it is sand mat, with its loathsome spines. This sand-covering plant appears as an innocent prostrate herb with dense leafy stems extending in all directions. The new shoots are quite flexible, and deer and rabbits eat them, but the tips of the sepals soon harden into formidable sharp spines that can easily penetrate the skin of man or beast. Walking on this plant is like walking over open rolls of barbed wire. Just finding the small barbs in my dog's paws is difficult, and attempting to remove them is quite a challenge.

The spines on the separate calyx segments that surround the embedded minute white florets make it almost impossible to examine the blooms. Aside from this plant's spines and prostrate growth habit, it grows fully exposed on the sand under the hot summer sun, which is probably why few insect herbivores occur on it. Yet yellowish gall gnat larvae live in the leaf sheaths, and beetle mites occur in the small flowers.

SAND MAT COMMUNITY
Herbivores
Gall gnat
Beetle mite
White-tailed deer
Brush rabbit

SAND MAT
(Cardionema ramosissimum:
Caryophyllaceae)
Characteristics: A smooth to finely
pubescent, tufted, prostrate perennial.
The white flowers are minute. The calyx
is composed of five unequal sepals, each
bearing a sharp spine at the tip. The small,
narrow leaves also have pointed tips.
Habitat and range: Along the Pacific
coast from Washington to Baja California.
Comments: The new growth is soft and
flexible, but as the plants mature, the
sepals and leaves harden and become
spine tipped and treacherous.

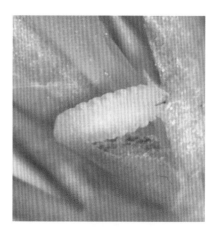

GALL GNAT
(Diptera: Cecidomyiidae)
Characteristics: The small larvae are
yellowish and elliptical, with black mouth
hooks. Adult gnats are small and black,
with clear wings and long legs.
Habitat and range: Dunes in Oregon.
Comments: Living within the base of
the leaf sheaths protects the larvae from
predators.

BEETLE MITE
(Phauloppia sp.: Oribatida: Oribatulidae)
Characteristics: Small brown mite with
a teardrop-shaped body. Legs tan, slender,
bearing short spines.
Habitat and range: Dunes in Oregon.
Comments: Large numbers of these
mites are associated with the flowers of
sand mat. Members of this mite family
are known to serve as intermediate
hosts of tapeworms (Anoplocephalidae:
Platyhelminthes). The adult tapeworms
occur in rabbits and other small
herbivores.

SEASIDE DAISY

Seaside daisy is one of the most attractive dune flowers, and its colors beautify the dunes from southern California to central Oregon. The outer rim of long pinkish petals encloses the inner circle of yellow florets. This color combination attracts a number of flower insects, including red-backed four-spotted longhorn beetles. Whether longhorn beetles are important pollinators of seaside daisy is questionable, but other insects, such as bumblebees, are just that.

One of the most fascinating flower visitors is the sand dune wasp, which actually looks more like a bee than a wasp. Sand dune wasps are hyperactive creatures that dart from flower to flower and plunge their long proboscis deep in the florets to find nectar. Between visiting flowers, they will suddenly alight on the sand and remain perfectly still under the summer sun. The females are always searching for flies. When they spot one, it takes only a split second for them to pounce on their prey, paralyze it with their stinger, and carry the unfortunate victim back to the nest as food for their brood. Flies aren't that easy to find, but the huge eyes of the sand dune wasp spot them easily. It is amazing that the females can relocate their covered nests in the sand after flying some distance away in search of more flies. Yellow jackets and purplish copper butterflies also come to the flowers for nectar and pollen.

Other insect herbivores live within the flower heads. Especially abundant are red-striped plume moth caterpillars, which feed on the developing seeds. They rarely expose themselves, and even the pupae are formed deep in the flower heads. Adult plume moths are quite striking with their narrow, outstretched wings expanded at the tips. What is especially intriguing is that their hind wings are cleft so deeply that they appear to be three separate wings. This wing structure does not seem to give them a flying advantage, though; their flight is slow and somewhat irregular.

Plume moth caterpillars share their habitat with a smaller flower caterpillar, the flower-head fly, and the flower inchworm. The slender, green-striped flower inchworm prefers to feed on the surface of the flower head and is active at night. During the day, it rests on the stems, using its body pattern as camouflage.

SEASIDE DAISY COMMUNITY
Herbivores
Four-spotted longhorn beetle
Bumblebees
Sand dune wasp
Yellow jackets
Purplish copper butterfly
Plume moth
Flower caterpillar
Flower-head fly
Flower inchworm

SEASIDE DAISY

(*Erigeron glaucus*: Asteraceae)

Characteristics: Small, compact, perennial daisy with clusters of entire or slightly toothed basal leaves and a series of leafy flower stems. Flowers with petal-like violet-lavender ray florets and yellowish disk florets.

Habitat and range: Dunes and coastal bluffs in Oregon and California.

Comments: Seaside daisy flowers from April through August.

FOUR-SPOTTED LONGHORN BEETLE

(*Anastrangalia laetifica*: Coleoptera: Cerambycidae)

Characteristics: Midsized, long-bodied beetles. Males are black except for bright red wing covers, each bearing two black spots. Females are completely black.

Habitat and range: Widely distributed in Canada, the United States, and Mexico.

Comments: This beetle is also called "dimorphic longhorn beetle" because of the different color patterns on the two sexes. The adults visit flowers for pollen and nectar.

SAND DUNE WASP

(*Bembix americana*: Hymenoptera: Crabronidae)

Characteristics: Midsized, hairy black wasp with broad white or yellowish bands on the abdomen, yellow legs, and large spherical eyes.

Habitat and range: Dunes from Washington to California and elsewhere.

Comments: The females are excellent diggers and excavate holes in the sand for their nests. The young are fed freshly caught flies that are stung and paralyzed. Sand dune wasps extend their mouthparts to obtain nectar from flowers. The females can deliver a painful sting.

PURPLISH COPPER BUTTERFLY

(*Epidemia helloides*: Lepidoptera: Lycaenidae)

Characteristics: Midsized butterfly with copper-brown wings with scattered black spots and dark margins. Caterpillars green, with longitudinal yellow stripes.

Habitat and range: Pacific coast from Canada to Mexico and inland.

Comments: These hardy butterflies remain until late fall, after most of the other coastal butterflies have disappeared. Caterpillars also develop on beach knotweed and seaside dock.

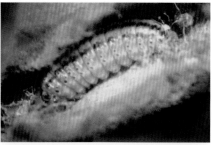

PLUME MOTH

(*Platyptilia williamsii*: Lepidoptera: Pterophoridae)

Characteristics: Caterpillar cream colored, with three reddish lines running the length of the body. Pupa tan, with longitudinal brown lines on abdomen; formed free, not in cocoon. Adult moth large, slender, brownish gray, with long legs and antennae and narrow, dark brown wings with cleft tips.

Habitat and range: Dunes in Oregon and California.

Comments: The caterpillars feed in the flower heads and are hidden from view. The adults sometimes look like aircraft with their long, outstretched wings.

FLOWER CATERPILLAR

(Lepidoptera: Tortricidae)

Characteristics: Caterpillars small, brownish, with a black pronotum and head.

Habitat and range: Dunes in Oregon and California.

Comments: The caterpillars feed on the developing seeds, thereby forming pathways through the yellow disk florets.

FLOWER-HEAD FLY

(*Tephritis* sp.: Diptera: Tephritidae)

Characteristics: Adults small, gray, with metallic-green eyes and pale wings blotched with black markings. Larvae white, puparia dark brown, both embedded in flower heads.

Habitat and range: Dunes in Oregon and California.

Comments: The metallic eyes of the adults are quite striking. The larvae feed on the developing seeds.

FLOWER INCHWORM

(Lepidoptera: Geometridae)

Characteristics: Caterpillars large, light greenish, with a tan head capsule and a series of horizontal dark lines.

Habitat and range: Dunes in Oregon and California.

Comments: The caterpillars are called inchworms because they bend their body upward and then extend the anterior portion, thus appearing to "inch" along.

ICE PLANT

The red-flowered sea fig and its yellow-flowered relative, the Hottentot fig, collectively known as ice plants, can be quite abundant on coastal dunes, especially in California. Hottentot fig has been widely planted along freeways, since it is little affected by smog, doesn't require much watering, and produces colorful flowers. In fact, Hottentot fig has often been referred to as the "freeway ice plant." When scale insects were inadvertently introduced into California from South Africa, there were mixed feelings. Highway workers wanted the scales killed to protect plantings along freeways, but ecologists wishing to get rid of the invasive ice plants in dune areas welcomed the scales. In the end, the highway people won and a program was initiated to biologically control the scale insects with parasitic wasps.

Cutting off and throwing away the branches does not kill ice plants because the cut portions put down roots. Pulling the plants up by the roots is almost impossible because they are very heavy and well rooted. Deer and rabbits eat the seeds and spread the plants throughout large areas of the dunes. Ice plants have been eradicated by hand from entire sections of the Humboldt dunes in order to provide space for native flora.

ICE PLANT COMMUNITY		
Herbivores	Parasites	Predators
White-tailed deer	Wasps	Ashy gray ladybird beetle
Brush rabbit		
Ice plant scale		

SEA FIG

(*Carpobrotus chilensis*: Aizoaceae)
Characteristics: A sprawling, aggressive perennial with medium-sized, rose to magenta flowers borne at the branch tips and fleshy, smooth-edged, opposite, triangular leaves.
Habitat and range: Dunes in California and southern Oregon.
Comments: Whether sea fig is native to California or was introduced from South Africa is still uncertain, but it is well adapted to conditions along the California coast.

HOTTENTOT FIG

(*Carpobrotus edulis*: Aizoaceae)

Characteristics: An aggressive sprawling perennial with yellow flowers borne at the branch tips and fleshy, sharp-edged, opposite, triangular leaves. Flowers may become pinkish later.

Habitat and range: Throughout California. Plants may occur in southern Oregon but usually suffer from excessive cold and moisture.

Comments: Hottentot fig is native to South Africa and was planted as a sand stabilizer for erosion control, especially along highways. However, it is quite invasive and will overgrow native plants, so there are now programs to eradicate it from dune areas. Hottentot fig will hybridize with sea fig, producing many intermediate forms.

SLENDER-LEAVED ICE PLANT

(*Conicosia pugioniformis*: Aizoaceae)

Characteristics: Flowers yellow, similar to those of Hottentot fig, but leaves are alternate, basal, and tube-shaped rather than opposite, attached to stems, and triangular.

Habitat and range: Restricted to dunes in central and northern California.

Comments: Slender-leaved ice plant is also native to South Africa, and although it is invasive, its distribution is much more limited than that of Hottentot fig and sea fig.

ICE PLANT SCALE

(*Pulvinariella mesembryanthemi*: Hemiptera: Coccidae)

Characteristics: Adult females small, first green, later becoming brown and surrounded with thick deposits of cottony white wax.

Habitat and range: Throughout dune and other arid habitats in California.

Comments: The large brown females deposit clusters of powdery white eggs within the white wax and then die. A related soft scale also on ice plant is *Pulvinaria delottoi*. Ice plant scale is parasitized by tiny wasps (Encyrtidae) and preyed on by ashy gray ladybird beetles (Coccinellidae).

ASHY GRAY LADYBIRD BEETLE

(*Olla v-nigrum*: Coleoptera: Coccinellidae)

Characteristics: A small ladybird beetle that occurs in several color variants, one of which is characterized by a single brick-red spot on each wing cover. Another color pattern is black spots on a light background.

Habitat and range: This beetle is widespread throughout most of North America and feeds on a variety of small insects, including ice plant scale as well as other scales and aphids.

Comments: When threatened by predators, the beetle can emit a bitter chemical from its leg joints.

GIANT VETCH

Giant vetch usually grows in tangled masses, with individual plants reaching several feet or more in length. The plants often have dune ants crawling over them searching for the nectary gland at the base of the flowers. This gland exudes a liquid that the ants obviously relish. Such extrafloral nectaries are found in a number of plants but are rarely placed at the base of flowers. By attracting ants, the giant vetch receives protection from leaf-feeding herbivores such as caterpillars, which are one of the ants' favorite food items. The presence of ants explains why most insect herbivores on giant vetch are concealed in plant tissue. Dune ant nests are often found close to giant vetch plants. The nests, which are constructed with plant material, especially small pieces of grass stems, can reach six feet across and one foot in height. Ant nests are a world unto themselves and harbor a range of symbionts and parasites. One of the latter is a wasp that cruises over the nest looking for ants to parasitize. The attack comes at lightning speed as the wasp alights and plunges its ovipositor into an ant. The deposited wasp egg produces a larva that will eat the insides of the ant, eventually emerging as a fleshy white larva ready to pupate. An ant predator is the larva of the red-backed clown beetle, which attacks immature ant stages in the nest. The colorful adults often rest exposed on the sand.

Ant symbionts come in many different shapes and sizes. One is an ant cricket that lives inside the nest and appears to groom the ants and feed on their products. Then there are microscopic nematodes that live in the ants' environment and produce a resistant, nonfeeding stage that enters the ants' salivary glands. The nematodes can be transferred from ant to ant during trophallaxis (the exchange of regurgitated digestive products between two ants). The nematodes eventually leave the ants and develop to maturity in the ant nest.

Female gall gnats inject chemicals into plant tissues to make them suitable as a home and food source for their young. In the case of the giant vetch gall gnat, the secretions cause a leaf to curl so tightly that it can't be straightened without breaking it apart. This makes an ideal safe house for the larvae and pupae of the gall gnat.

The larvae of the leaf-bud weevil are concealed deep within the plant's tissue during their development. It is curious that the bud weevil larvae are decorated with irregular brown bands, because they develop out of sight where they would not require any protective coloring.

GIANT VETCH COMMUNITY		
Herbivores	Parasites/Predators	Symbionts
Dune ant	Dune ant wasp	Ant cricket
Gall gnat	Red-backed clown beetle	Dune ant nematode
Leaf-bud weevil		

GIANT VETCH
(*Vicia gigantea*: Fabaceae)

Characteristics: Robust sprawling and climbing perennial with leaves divided into numerous (up to twenty-eight) leaflets. Leaf tips bearing simple to branched tendrils. Flowers numerous, initially pink, then turning brown, borne in one-sided clusters on long, leafless stalks.

Habitat and range: Dunes from Washington to California.

Comments: At the base of many flowers is a dark reddish nectary gland whose secretions attract dune ants (lower photo).

DUNE ANT

(*Formica obscuriventris clivia*:
Hymenoptera: Formicidae)

Characteristics: Small black ant with a
reddish-brown thorax and large red head.
Habitat and range: Dunes and wood-
lands from Washington to California.
Comments: Dune ants are common all
along the coast, especially in Oregon and
Washington. They construct large nests
from stems of various plants, especially
grasses. The workers forage for food, especially caterpillars, and nest construction
material. Many organisms are associated
with dune ants and their nests.

DUNE ANT WASP

(*Elasmosoma ruthe*: Hymenoptera: Braconidae)

Characteristics: Extremely small brown wasp with antennae as long as its abdomen and a pronounced dark spot (stigma) on each forewing.

Habitat and range: Dunes from Washington to California.

Comments: The female wasp maneuvers skillfully, flying just above the ants and then suddenly dashing down and inserting an egg in an ant's abdomen. The egg develops into a white larva that eventually leaves the dying ant and pupates in the sand near the ant nest. Sometimes an ant being chased by a wasp will suddenly turn around and catch it in its mandibles (center).

RED-BACKED CLOWN BEETLE

(*Spilodiscus sellatus*: Coleoptera:
Histeridae)

Characteristics: Midsized shiny black
beetle with a thick armored body wall and
a large red area on each wing cover.
Habitat and range: Dunes from
Washington to California.
Comments: The adults are usually well
hidden in the sand, while the larvae live
in ant nests and feed on ant larvae.

ANT CRICKET

(*Myrmecophila* sp.: Orthoptera: Gryllidae)
Characteristics: Small, wingless brown
cricket with a smooth, oval body, short
legs, and thin antennae.
Habitat and range: Dunes from
Washington to California.
Comments: These crickets inhabit the
nests of dune ants and have attributes that
allow them to enter and survive in these
"hostile" environments. They obtain food
by licking the ants' bodies, which makes
the ants regurgitate their last meal.

DUNE ANT NEMATODE

(*Pristionchus* sp.: Rhabditida:
Diplogastridae)
Characteristics: Microscopic, slender
worm lacking segments, with a rounded
head and pointed tail.
Habitat and range: Dunes from
Washington to California.
Comments: The resting stage of these
nematodes occurs in the esophageal
glands of ants. Upon the death of an ant,
the nematodes develop on the remains.

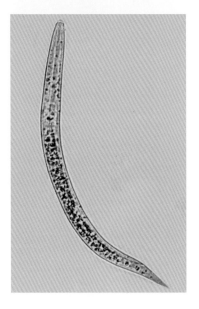

GALL GNAT

(*Dasineura* sp.: Diptera: Cecidomyiidae)

Characteristics: Adult gnat small, brown, with dark head, fuscous wings, and long legs. Larva legless, white. Pupa forms in a silken cocoon inside gall.

Habitat and range: Dunes from Washington to California.

Comments: The larvae live inside rolled leaves. This is one of the gall gnats that pupate in silken cocoons.

LEAF-BUD WEEVIL

(*Apion* sp.: Coleoptera: Brentidae)

Characteristics: Larva small, legless, curved, white with reddish-brown pattern on back. Adult small, black, with some white scales over the body.

Habitat and range: Dunes from Washington to California.

Comments: The larvae feed on the developing leaf buds, so that when the leaves open, they have symmetrical holes on both sides.

POISON OAK

Poison oak is one plant you want to avoid, and while I have never found it growing in the coastal dunes of Oregon and Washington, it is fairly common along most of the California coast, especially in the south. So the big question is, why doesn't this plant populate the entire coast of the Pacific Northwest? It can't be the cold winters, since poison oak grows along the Eastern Seaboard where temperatures drop well below freezing. Even though poison oak can cause a serious dermatitis reaction in humans, white-tailed deer and rabbits will eat the foliage.

One interesting invertebrate herbivore that appears to be a specialist feeder on this plant is a minute gall mite. Living within bright red galls that stand out like drops of blood on the green leaves, these tiny mites imbibe the sap. Their bodies are so modified that it is difficult to recognize them as mites. They look more like some type of insect larvae. In addition, while most mites, depending on their maturity, have eyes and six or eight legs, these creatures are blind and have only two legs. At a particular time in their development, they leave their red galls and wait on the leaf for the wind to carry them off to another poison oak plant.

POISON OAK COMMUNITY
Herbivores
White-tailed deer
Brush rabbit
Gall mite

POISON OAK
(*Toxicodendron diversilobum*: Anacardiaceae)
Characteristics: A deciduous plant that can be in the form of a vine, shrub, or small tree. Leaves divided into three (sometimes five) irregularly lobed leaflets. Leaves turn reddish in autumn. Flowers small, greenish yellow; fruits greenish at first, then become white.
Habitat and range: Dunes in California and inland.
Comments: I never found poison oak in the dune systems of Oregon and Washington.

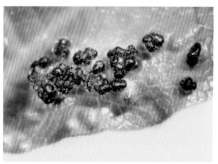

GALL MITE

(*Aculops rhois:* Acari: Eriophyidae)

Characteristics: Very small mite with a soft, yellowish, elongated body and only two pairs of anteriorly placed legs.

Habitat and range: Dunes in California and inland.

Comments: The swollen, irregular red galls on the leaves of poison oak are a reaction of the plant to the feeding mites. The mites are dispersed by wind.

BEACH PRIMROSE

Beach primrose blends in against the sand when not in flower. It is curious that this little plant prefers to grow in full sun yet folds up its beautiful yellow petals late in the afternoon. The seedpods of beach primrose are strongly curved and look at first like deformed leaves. The pod moth caterpillar chooses these pods as an ideal place to raise its young. Although the caterpillar is hidden inside the seedpod, a female wasp manages to insert her ovipositor through the pod wall, locate the caterpillar, and deposit an egg right on its body. The wasp larva remains on the surface of the victim, eventually consuming the entire caterpillar except for the black head capsule.

Black flea beetle larvae have also found a home with beach primrose. The hatchlings enter inside the tender new leaves, remaining hidden while feeding. When they outgrow these accommodations, they continue feeding on the leaf surfaces. They need to eat quickly before a predator spots their dark outlines.

BEACH PRIMROSE COMMUNITY	
Herbivores	Parasites
Bees	Pod moth wasp
Pod moth	
Flea beetle	

BEACH PRIMROSE

(*Camissonia cheiranthifolia*: Onagraceae)

Characteristics: Hairy, short-lived perennial with mostly prostrate stems radiating out from a central rosette. The pubescent oval leaves are covered with a "bloom." The four yellow petals close in the late afternoon or evening. The mature flower pods are tightly curled.

Habitat and range: Dunes from Oregon to Baja California.

Comments: The flowers of beach primrose are visited by several types of bees. Beach primrose is sensitive to crowding and cold, wet winters and usually survives only a few years in most locations.

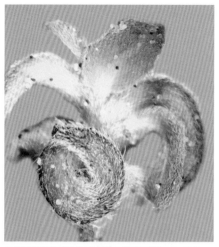

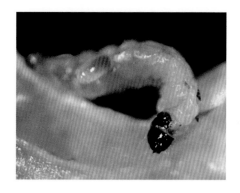

POD MOTH

(*Mompha* sp.: Lepidoptera: Momphidae)

Characteristics: The small pale caterpillar has a black head and pronotum. The small adult moth is white with various brown scale patterns on its wings.

Habitat and range: Dunes in Oregon and California.

Comments: The caterpillars develop within the curved seedpods of beach primrose. A parasitic wasp (Hymenoptera: Braconidae) may deposit one or two eggs on a caterpillar. Upon hatching, the wasp larvae consume the caterpillar from the outside (ectoparasitic).

FLEA BEETLE

(*Altica* sp.: Coleoptera: Chrysomelidae)

Characteristics: Larvae are small, olive green to brown, with a series of black tubercles on each body segment and a black head and legs.

Habitat and range: Dunes in Oregon and California.

Comments: The conspicuous dark larvae feed on the leaves, and as hatchlings they will first enter inside the leaves and feed between the leaf surfaces.

COAST BUCKWHEAT

Visit the Humboldt Bay dunes in northern California in late spring to see a wonderful display of the beautiful pink flowers of coast buckwheat. A large area of the dunes that has been cleared of marram grass now supports the round flower clusters of this native plant. The flowers attract various pollinators, including mason bees. But these bees don't just collect pollen; they carefully scrape off the downy hairs on the leaves, which they use to line their nests.

All that hard work establishing a nest may be for nothing if a female velvet ant wasp locates it and decides to deposit her own eggs near the bee progeny. The velvet ant's thick body wall protects it from female leaf-cutter bees, and the absence of wings allows the wasp to easily enter the bee's nest. Male velvet ants are quite different from the females: not only are they larger and differently colored, but they also possess wings.

Mimicry is a fantastic device that allows a defenseless organism to imitate one that is armed against predators. Some scarabs on coast buckwheat are quite hairy, possess exposed abdomens, and imitate the motions of bumblebees. These bumblebee scarabs even mimic the flight patterns of bumblebees, but not the speed. These impersonations safeguard the beetles as they feed on the flowers of coast buckwheat, since few predators want to tangle with bumblebees.

Other beetles, such as flea beetles, prefer the leaves of coast buckwheat, and their disguise is to imitate excrement deposited on the leaves. Later, these unsavory-appearing larvae transform into beautiful, glistening, metallic-green flea beetles with powerful hind legs. These remarkable limbs are capable of rapidly propelling the insects away from predators.

Inchworm caterpillars have a different type of mimicry: instead of acting like another insect, they imitate plant parts. When the foliage of coast buckwheat is disturbed, short branches suddenly appear to be growing out of some of the stems. These branches don't move when touched and appear genuine. However, they are rigid inchworm caterpillars mimicking the stems of coast buckwheat. Each caterpillar has a pair of basal legs firmly attached to the plant stem. The rest of its rigid body appears smooth since the true walking legs are tightly held under its head. To avoid any suspicion that it is a caterpillar, it extends its body at an angle resembling that of a stem, and to look completely natural, it positions itself upside down!

COAST BUCKWHEAT COMMUNITY	
Herbivores	**Parasites**
Mason bee	Velvet ant
Yellow-haired bumblebee scarab	Red-tipped wasp
Brown-haired bumblebee scarab	Bee mites
Acmon blue butterfly	
Flea beetle	
Yellow-spotted moth	
Inchworm	
Plume moth	
Cutworm	

COAST BUCKWHEAT
(*Eriogonum latifolium*: Polygonaceae)

Characteristics: Perennial plant with a deep taproot and dense, basal, white-woolly leaves. Flowering stems leafless, sometimes forked, bearing terminal clusters of pinkish flowers.

Habitat and range: Dunes, sea bluffs, and rocky ledges in California and Oregon.

Comments: The flowers are visited by a variety of pollinators.

MASON BEE

(*Anthidium* sp.: Hymenoptera: Megachilidae)

Characteristics: Small black bee with transverse white lines on abdominal segments. Head and thorax bearing long hairs. Pollen is carried in the stiff hairs on the underside of the abdomen.

Habitat and range: Dunes in California and Oregon.

Comments: Mason bees visit the flowers for nectar and pollen but also remove the fuzzy hairs from the leaves to line their nests. Parasitic mites are sometimes attached to the bees.

VELVET ANT

(*Dasymutilla* sp.: Hymenoptera: Mutillidae)

Characteristics: Female velvet ants are midsized, wingless, and covered with long reddish hairs. Male velvet ants are larger than the females, winged, and usually dark with short body hairs.

Habitat and range: Dunes in California and Oregon and elsewhere.

Comments: The females are diurnal and deposit their eggs in the ground nests of bees and wasps, including leaf-cutter bees. After destroying their host, the velvet ant larvae form a cocoon in the victim's nest.

YELLOW-HAIRED BUMBLEBEE SCARAB

(*Lichnanthe ursina*: Coleoptera: Glaphyridae)

Characteristics: A stout, midsized, yellow- to orange-haired scarab with brownish white-spotted wing covers (elytra) that are shorter than the abdomen.

Habitat and range: Dunes in California.

Comments: The adults feed on nectar and pollen and the larvae develop on living and decaying plant matter in the soil. The adults are clumsy fliers and their survival is probably due to their resemblance to bumblebees, since their slow flight makes them easy targets for birds.

BROWN-HAIRED BUMBLEBEE SCARAB

(*Lichnanthe rathvoni*: Coleoptera: Glaphyridae)

Characteristics: A stout, midsized, mostly brown-haired scarab with brownish white-lined wing covers that are shorter than the abdomen. The thorax bears long light-yellow hairs.

Habitat and range: Dunes from Washington to California as well as inland.

Comments: Like the yellow-haired bumblebee scarab, the brown-haired bumblebee scarab visits flowers for nectar and pollen. This species has a much wider distribution along the coast than the yellow-haired bumblebee scarab.

ACMON BLUE BUTTERFLY

(*Icaricia acmon*: Lepidoptera: Lycaenidae)

Characteristics: Caterpillars short and flattened; brown, green, or slightly purplish. Adults large, each sex with different coloration. Undersides of female wings light gray to brown, with black spots and a row of orange crescents along the outer margins of the hind wings. Males have blue wings with dark edges.

Habitat and range: Dunes in California and Oregon.

Comments: The caterpillars feed on the leaves and the adults visit the flowers.

FLEA BEETLE

(*Altica* sp.: Coleoptera: Chrysomelidae)

Characteristics: Larvae short, stubby, dark brown to black. Adults small, shiny metallic green, with thick hind femora and long black antennae.

Habitat and range: Dunes in California and Oregon.

Comments: The larvae feed on the leaves and the adults browse both leaves and flowers.

YELLOW-SPOTTED MOTH

(*Chionodes* sp.: Lepidoptera: Gelechiidae)

Characteristics: Caterpillars yellowish to pinkish, with a black head capsule. Adults brown, with small yellow spots on the forewings and elongated scales on the wing tips.

Habitat and range: Dunes in California.

Comments: The caterpillars feed on the leaves. *Chionodes* is a large genus, and several species are known to feed on coast buckwheat.

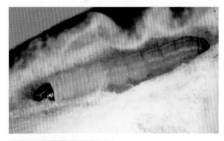

INCHWORM
(Lepidoptera: Geometridae)

Characteristics: Large, light brown caterpillar with dark brown blotches and only two pairs of pseudopods (false legs) at the base of the body. At rest, the three pairs of true legs are held tightly against the body.
Habitat and range: Dunes in California and Oregon.
Comments: When disturbed, the caterpillars extend their body and remain motionless, resembling a broken-off sprig. They are usually oriented with their back to the ground.

PLUME MOTH
(Lepidoptera: Pterophoridae)

Characteristics: Caterpillars with alternating white and brown or reddish stripes running the length of the body. Adult moths large and tan, with long, narrow wings and long legs.
Habitat and range: Dunes in California and Oregon.
Comments: The caterpillars feed only on the flowers and are usually hidden within the petals. They are attacked by the red-tipped wasp.

RED-TIPPED WASP
(*Atanycolus* sp.: Hymenoptera: Braconidae)

Characteristics: Large, elongated black wasp with a red-tipped abdomen. The female has an ovipositor as long as her body.
Habitat and range: Dunes in California and Oregon.
Comments: These wasps are diurnal, and females insert their long ovipositor into plume moth caterpillars hiding among the flowers. The larvae are internal parasites. Adult wasps feed on nectar.

CUTWORM
(*Peridroma* sp.: Lepidoptera: Noctuidae)

Characteristics: Large, light brown caterpillar with three irregular, broken dark bands running the length of the body.
Habitat and range: Dunes in California and Oregon.
Comments: These cutworms develop in the flower clusters and curl up when disturbed. They are generalist feeders.

YELLOW WALLFLOWER

Yellow wallflower is a striking plant, with its cluster of yellow flowers borne at the top of a straight leafy stem. The leaves are long at the base but become shorter as they ascend toward the flowers.

This endangered plant is rapidly disappearing, and attempts are being made to preserve it on California dunes. Hastening its disappearance is a small caterpillar that feeds on the stiff seedpods that protrude from the stems. Many pods are infected with these caterpillars, but their presence does not deter the deer that dine on the pods during the night. These caterpillars often rest on the tips of the pods, which is probably not prudent since small wasps search for them there.

Two types of weevil also occur on the pods. The chunky pod weevil has an interesting escape mechanism. When approached, it pulls in its legs and tumbles to the ground, no matter how high it is on the plant. The seed weevil has a different escape tactic. It freezes in its tracks, digs its claws into the plant tissue, and pretends it has been turned to stone.

A rather unsightly white rust fungus adds insult to injury on wallflower stems. The raised pale blisters coalesce into tumorlike bodies that can eventually destroy the plant. Microscopic spore balls that transmit the disease cover the mature fungus layer.

The wallflower is considered a six-year perennial, in which only vegetative growth occurs during the first five years, slowly building up enough food to support the flowering stem on the sixth year, after which the plant dies. This long vegetative period before reproduction may have a bearing on why this plant is endangered. The longer a plant takes to reproduce, the more time it is exposed to predation and diseases, thus lessening its chances of survival.

YELLOW WALLFLOWER COMMUNITY	
Herbivores	Parasites
Pod moth	Pod moth wasp
Pod weevil	White rust
Seed weevil	
Small milkweed bug	
Aphid	
Flea beetle	
Sand treader	
White-tailed deer	

YELLOW WALLFLOWER

(*Erysimum menziesii*: Brassicaceae)

Characteristics: A six-year perennial with a cluster of elongated basal leaves in a dense rosette, and usually a single stem terminating in a cluster of bright yellow flowers. Seedpods (fruits) are long, narrow, perpendicular to the stem, and straight or curled slightly upward at the apex.

Habitat and range: Dune areas in California.

Comments: The flowering period is March and April. This species, which is also known as the Humboldt Bay wallflower, is represented by only four populations (or subspecies) in California. Three of these are listed as endangered because of habitat loss. The effect of the herbivores shown here on the survival of yellow wallflower has not been evaluated. Deer also browse on the flowers and seedpods.

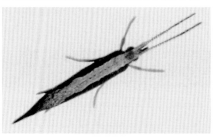

POD MOTH

(*Plutella* sp.: Lepidoptera: Plutellidae)

Characteristics: The midsized, grayish-green caterpillars live within the pods and feed on the developing seeds. The midsized, slender brown moths have a longitudinal row of light scales along their back.

Habitat and range: Dunes in California and possibly elsewhere in North America.

Comments: The caterpillars initially begin feeding inside the pods but, as they grow, shift their activities to the surface of the pods, where they are subject to parasitism by small wasps (Hymenoptera: Braconidae). The caterpillars and adults resemble those of the diamondback moth, which attacks sea rocket, but the color patterns on the backs of the adults differ.

POD WEEVIL
(*Ceutorhynchus* sp.: Coleoptera: Curculionidae)

Characteristics: Small, short, stubby dark brown beetle with patches of white scales on the wing covers. Underside and legs covered with white scales. The long beak can be brought down into a groove under the head. The white, legless, C-shaped larvae develop inside the seedpods.
Habitat and range: Dunes in California.
Comments: The adults are quite sensitive to vibrations and use falling as an escape mechanism.

SEED WEEVIL
(*Apion* sp.: Coleoptera: Brentidae)

Characteristics: Small, narrow brown weevil with a nearly straight beak. Scattered pale scales occur over the body. The larvae are small, white, and legless.
Habitat and range: Dunes in California.
Comments: The larvae feed on the developing seeds.

SMALL MILKWEED BUG
(*Lygaeus kalmii*: Hemiptera: Lygaeidae)

Characteristics: Adult midsized, green-ish, with a small red spot on the head and black spots and orange markings on the thorax and wing covers. Tips of wings black, with a narrow white margin and white spots.
Habitat and range: Coastal dunes and elsewhere in North America.
Comments: This is a generalist feeder that consists of several strains, each with a slightly different color pattern.

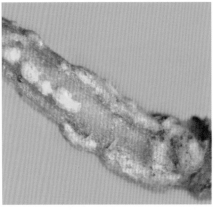

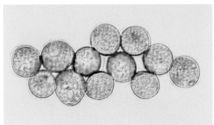

WHITE RUST

(*Albugo candida*: Oomycetes: Albuginaceae)

Characteristics: White rust forms yellowish, tumorlike bodies on the stems of yellow wallflower. The fungus develops inside the host cells, eventually forming round to oval sporangia.

Habitat and range: There are many strains of this fungus. This one occurs on yellow wallflower in California dunes.

Comments: Heavy infections can affect plant growth and survival.

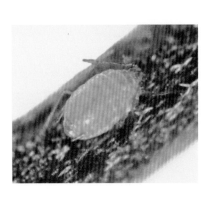

APHID

(*Lipaphis erysimi*: Hemiptera: Aphididae)

Characteristics: Small, pale green aphid with long antennae and medium-sized cornicles.

Habitat and range: Widespread throughout North America.

Comments: These aphids, which are not abundant, belong to a wide-ranging species group that attacks members of the mustard family (Brassicaceae).

FLEA BEETLE

(*Altica* sp.: Coleoptera: Chrysomelidae)

Characteristics: Adults are small, shiny black, with thick hind femora. Larvae are also black and have a somewhat wrinkled appearance.

Habitat and range: Dunes in California.

Comments: Both larvae and adults feed on yellow wallflower. The adults can jump quite rapidly with their muscular hind legs.

SAND TREADER

(*Rhachocnemis validus*: Orthoptera: Gryllacrididae)

Characteristics: A large, light brown insect with short antennae, no wings, and hind legs equipped with long spurs for moving through sand.

Habitat and range: Dunes in California, especially in southern California.

Comments: These nocturnal insects are also known as beach camel crickets and spend most of the day buried in the sand. They do not produce audible sounds. The leg spurs can be quite painful when handled. They occur in sand around some populations of yellow wallflower, but their effect on these plants is not known.

BEACH MORNING GLORY

Everyone is familiar with the common morning glory, but most don't know that there is another species that lives in the dunes. Stems of the beach morning glory lie on the sand, and their small, thick, kidney-shaped leaves rarely rise more than a few inches from the surface. The open, pink to purple or lavender flowers are almost as large as those of the garden variety of our common morning glory. In the early morning, dew collects on the petals, each droplet reflecting the brilliance of the sun. Eventually the drips coalesce and move to the edge of the petals, where they fall off and disappear in the sand. Near a cluster of plants, the scent from the flowers is delightful, and visiting hummingbirds and butterflies indicate there is a good nectar supply. The flowers respond to the weather conditions, remaining closed on wet days and open in fair weather.

Small, sausage-shaped plume moth caterpillars quietly chew away on the leaves of beach morning glory. Their entire body supports clusters of branched, pointed spines, and any predator would hesitate before attacking such a spiny creature. The long-legged, narrow-winged adult moths are quite gangly after emerging from their streamlined pupal case. While fluttering around the flowers for nectar, the plume moths may encounter stocky dune scarabs that relish the blooms.

Some of the flowers contain red dots that move this way and that and then collect at the base near the nectar supply. It wasn't until I had one of these creatures under the microscope that I recognized it as a red flower mite. Its color is so brilliant that the mite appears to have been dipped in a can of bright red paint. Perhaps the color is an indication of its disposition, since this mite is very territorial and will even bite humans if they get in the way.

BEACH MORNING GLORY COMMUNITY
Herbivores
Plume moth
Dune scarab beetle
Red flower mite
Mealybug
Sand dune weevil
Hummingbirds
Butterflies
Ants
Bumblebees

BEACH MORNING GLORY

(*Calystegia soldanella*: Convolvulaceae)

Characteristics: Large, showy, trumpet-shaped flowers with bracts subtending the calyx and pinkish-purple to white petals. Leaves thick, fleshy, kidney shaped. Stems prostrate, reaching up to eight feet in length, sometimes forming compact masses of vegetation.

Habitat and range: Sand dunes all along the Pacific coast.

Comments: Beach morning glory flowers are frequently visited by ants and bumblebees.

DUNE SCARAB BEETLE

(*Serica anthracina*: Coleoptera: Scarabaeidae)

Characteristics: Adult beetles are midsized and uniformly dark brown, with longitudinal striations on the wing covers. The grubs are white and curved, with a brown head.

Habitat and range: Dunes along the Pacific coast.

Comments: The adults feed on various flowers and make a buzzing sound during flight. The grubs feed on the roots of dune plants.

RED FLOWER MITE

(*Balaustium* sp.: Acarina: Erythraeidae)

Characteristics: Small, velvety red mites with eight legs, with the middle pairs of legs shorter than the front and back pairs.
Habitat and range: Members of this cosmopolitan genus occur in soil litter as well as on various plant parts, including bark, leaves, and flowers.
Comments: The mites move quite rapidly in the flower tubes of beach morning glory, where they feed on pollen and nectar. The adults are also predaceous (and cannibalistic) on small insects and attack mealybugs feeding on beach morning glory. Red flower mites are also known to bite humans, causing irritating pimples that can become infected.

PLUME MOTH

(*Emmelina monodactyla*: Lepidoptera: Pterophoridae)

Characteristics: The greenish-yellow caterpillar is covered with spinelike setae and has a faint dark band extending the length of the back. The pupa is slender and light brown, with black spots and clusters of setae on the back. The midsized adult moth is light brown, with some dark markings on the narrow forewings.
Habitat and range: Dunes along the Pacific Northwest coast.
Comments: Development is quite rapid, and there are probably several generations annually.

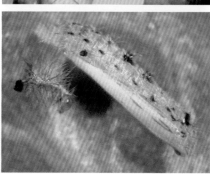

MEALYBUG

(*Pseudococcus* sp.: Hemiptera:
Pseudococcidae)

Characteristics: Immature feeding stages
are small, reddish, and partly covered with
white scales.

Habitat and range: Dunes in Oregon and
California.

Comments: These mealybugs live in
blotch mines that look like brownish leaf
spots.

SAND DUNE WEEVIL

(*Trigonoscuta pilosa*: Coleoptera:
Curculionidae)

Characteristics: Small, short-snouted
brownish-gray beetle covered with light
and dark scales.

Habitat and range: Occurs in dunes
from Washington to northern California.

Comments: These elusive weevils feed
and mate at night on a variety of dune
plants and are especially fond of floral
parts.

SCOTCH BROOM

The two-lipped yellow flowers of Scotch broom flanked by the dark green foliage are quite attractive. That was one of the reasons this woody shrub was introduced from Europe. Scotch broom was also considered a dune stabilizer and so was planted along a major portion of the Pacific coast. When it was discovered that the plants were spreading and hard to control, that livestock ignored them, and that they were displacing native flora, biological control agents were imported. The seeds of Scotch broom were considered a crucial target for control since they can remain viable for eighty years. One insect selected was a European seed weevil. The hope was that if enough seeds were killed, plant populations would be reduced. The weevils do eat the seeds, but Scotch broom retaliates by forming dark, tightly closed pods, so by the time the weevils are finished feeding, many are imprisoned and bake under the hot summer sun. Weevils that survive are those that can wait until the pods have dried and split open, spreading the contents over the sand.

In addition to this, the weevils have another problem. Two small metallic-blue native wasps decided that Scotch broom weevil larvae furnished a juicy meal and found a way to penetrate the seedpod and deposit their eggs on the weevil larvae. After hatching, the parasite larvae dine on the immature weevils.

And as if high temperatures and wasp parasites weren't enough, a pearl mite with a notorious record is also on the scene. Pearl mites care little about their type of prey and are known to even attack field workers. The tiny eight-legged adults don't look dangerous at first, but after the females attach themselves to weevil larvae and begin feeding, their small abdomen becomes so distended that their feet lose contact with the substrate. The bloated body becomes filled with eggs that will release young, thus spelling doom for any additional developing weevils. Sometimes, wasps and pearl mites choose the same weevil larva to attack.

Scotch Broom Community	
Herbivores	Parasites
Seed weevil	Wasps
Spt-winged bark louse	Pearl mite
	Gregarine protozoa

SCOTCH BROOM

(*Cytisus scoparius*: Fabaceae)

Characteristics: Woody, bushy perennial with numerous spreading branches, trifid leaves, and bright yellow, pealike flowers. Seedpods pealike, with up to eight seeds that become brown and quite hard at maturity.

Habitat and range: Dunes and inland from British Columbia to California. Introduced from Europe.

Comments: Scotch broom was planted as a sand stabilizer and rapidly spread to surrounding areas, becoming a serious pest. The seeds are quite resistant and can remain viable for years.

SEED WEEVIL

(*Exapion fuscirostre*: Coleoptera: Brentidae)

Characteristics: Adults small, pear shaped, grayish brown, with long, slender, pale scales and an almost straight beak. Pupae white, formed in seedpods. Larvae C-shaped, white, with a brown head capsule.

Habitat and range: Dunes along the west coast.

Comments: This weevil was released as a biological control agent of Scotch broom. It is fairly common in some areas, but populations are maintained at low levels in other areas by tightly closed pods as well as wasp and mite parasites.

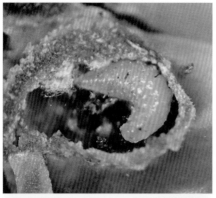

PARASITIC WASP
(*Pteromalus sequester*: Hymenoptera: Pteromalidae)

Characteristics: Larvae small, white, with a pointed head and blunt tail. Adult wasp small, stout, brownish, with a broad head as wide as the rest of the body, membranous wings, and a short, pointed abdomen with an iridescent sheen.

Habitat and range: Dunes in Oregon.

Comments: This wasp, along with the narrow-bodied eupelmid wasp (Hymenoptera: Eupelmidae, bottom), also parasitizes the larvae and pupae of the seed weevil.

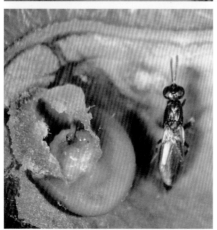

PEARL MITE

(*Pyemotes* sp.: Acarina: Pyemotidae)

Characteristics: Free-living adults are small and turtle shaped and have eight short legs bearing long setae. After the females feed, their abdomen enlarges and becomes pear shaped. The eggs hatch inside the enlarged abdomen, and the young complete their development in the same location. Mating occurs as soon as they emerge.

Habitat and range: Dunes in Oregon.

Comments: This species parasitizes larvae and pupae of the seed weevil. Some pearl mites attack humans and cause skin eruptions called "grain itch."

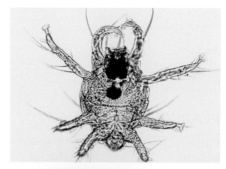

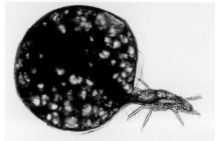

SPOT-WINGED BARK LOUSE

(*Ectopsocus californicus*: Psocomorpha: Ectopsocidae)

Characteristics: Small, fragile insect with large head, protruding eyes, long antennae, and dark spots on the membranous wings.

Habitat and range: Dunes from Washington to California.

Comments: Bark lice live inside partially open pods of Scotch broom and feed on the remaining debris. Gregarine protozoa develop in the gut cells and intestine of many bark lice in the pods (lower photo).

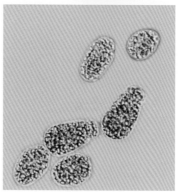

PEARLY EVERLASTING

Pearly everlasting is quite widespread in various parts of the world and has adapted to the dunes along the Pacific coast, where it is part of the ecology. Each mature flower of pearly everlasting looks like a round eyeball with a yellow iris and black pupil. Aside from a range of pollinators, including sweat bees, several insects have chosen the flowers of pearly everlasting as a food source for their young. A delicate spotted-wing fruit fly stops by the flowers to deposit a batch of small, barely perceptible white eggs. Soon afterward, wiggly white maggots appear among the flower heads or inside the stems. These eventually transform into dark, thick-walled, football-shaped puparia. The maggots jostle for space among the flowers with red-striped plume moth caterpillars, flower moth caterpillars, and flower weevils. Adult plume moths look like strange experimental aircraft with their long, narrow, outstretched forewings and three-lobed hind wings. Colonies of black aphids with two long tubes (cornicles) dot the stems of pearly everlasting in late summer. The tubes look like cannons and emit a waxy substance for defense. Unfortunately, this does not protect the aphids from parasitic wasps. The wasp larvae live inside the aphid, eventually turning it into a gray mummy that remains attached to the stem. When ready to emerge, the wasp cuts a circular hole through the back of the aphid and pushes open the hatch.

PEARLY EVERLASTING COMMUNITY	
Herbivores	Parasites
Sweat bee	Braconid wasp
Flower fly	
Plume moth	
Flower moth	
Flower weevil	
Aphids	

PEARLY EVERLASTING

(*Anaphalis margaritacea*: Asteraceae)

Characteristics: Perennial plants with rhizomes and narrow, alternate leaves that are green above and white woolly below, clasping at base. Yellow disk flowers in flat-topped clusters surrounded by pearly white, dry bracts on terminal stems.

Habitat and range: Coastal dunes from California to Alaska and inland.

Comments: The pearly white flower bracts retain their color and shape when dried.

SWEAT BEE

(*Agapostemon* sp.: Hymenoptera: Halictidae)

Characteristics: Midsized dark bee with striped abdomen and various degrees of metallic coloration on its body.

Habitat and range: Dunes from Washington to California.

Comments: These solitary bees usually build their nests in the ground. They visit various dune flowers for nectar and pollen.

FLOWER FLY

(*Trupanea californica*: Diptera: Tephritidae)

Characteristics: Small gray flies with iridescent eyes and membranous wings with a black, starlike pattern at the apices. Mature larvae are white with black mouth hooks. The puparia are elliptical and dark brown at maturity.

Habitat and range: Dunes from Washington to California and elsewhere in western North America.

Comments: The larvae develop in the flower ovaries and occasionally within the stems.

PLUME MOTH

(*Platyptilia* sp.: Lepidoptera: Pterophoridae)

Characteristics: Caterpillar pale, with dark brown head and pronotum and three broad red bands running along the back. Adult moth large, brownish, slender, with long legs and narrow extended forewings widened at the tips.

Habitat and range: Dunes from Washington to California.

Comments: The caterpillars, which destroy the developing seeds, are easy to recognize by their red stripes.

FLOWER MOTH

(Lepidoptera: Tortricidae)
Characteristics: Caterpillars cream colored, with dark brown head and pronotum.
Habitat and range: Dunes from Washington to California.
Comments: The caterpillars are deeply embedded within the flower heads. Adult moths were not obtained.

FLOWER WEEVIL

(*Tychius* sp.: Coleoptera: Curculionidae)
Characteristics: Small brown weevil covered with light gray scales.
Habitat and range: Dunes from Washington to California.
Comments: The adults are usually hidden within the flower clusters. Larvae were not recovered.

APHID

(*Uroleucon russellae*: Hemiptera: Aphididae)
Characteristics: Small, elongated, reddish-brown aphid with long legs often darkened at the joints.
Habitat and range: Various habitats in North America.
Comments: Heavy populations build up on pearly everlasting during the spring and summer. The swollen, light gray aphid in the photograph is parasitized by a wasp larva (Hymenoptera: Braconidae).

HOOKER'S EVENING PRIMROSE

The large yellow flowers of Hooker's evening primrose are quite striking in the dune environment. This plant reproduces quite well and in some areas forms dense thickets, with individual plants reaching four to five feet tall. There are a number of subspecies, and while considered a California native, it has spread up the coast and can be found in Washington and Oregon. Hooker's evening primrose is a prolific and invasive species that spreads rapidly by seed. Leaf rollers and aphids are the most common insects encountered on it.

HOOKER'S EVENING PRIMROSE COMMUNITY			
Herbivores		Scavengers	Parasites
Leaf roller		Earwig	Flower fly
Aphid			
Dune ant			

HOOKER'S EVENING PRIMROSE
(*Oenothera elata* subsp. *hookeri*: Onagraceae)
Characteristics: Large, erect, short-lived perennial with smooth to wrinkled hairy leaves attached to a thick, fibrous central stem. Flowers large, yellow, with four petals; borne on short stalks along upper portion of stem.
Habitat and range: Dunes from Washington to California.
Comments: The flower bases are especially attractive to earwigs.

LEAF ROLLER

(*Acleris* sp.: Lepidoptera: Tortricidae)

Characteristics: Caterpillars light green with a tan head. Adult moths small, yellowish, with dark brown bands on forewings.

Habitat and range: Dunes in Oregon.

Comments: This moth genus is widespread, and there are many variations in the color patterns on the wings.

APHID

(Hemiptera: Aphididae)

Characteristics: Small green aphids with rows of white (in immatures) or black (in winged adults) spots on their backs. Winged adults have dark heads, antennae, and wing veins.

Habitat and range: Dunes in Oregon.

Comments: These aphids appear to be restricted to Hooker's evening primrose on the dunes. Dune ants come to obtain honeydew from the aphids, and flower fly larvae (Diptera: Syrphidae) feed on the aphids.

COYOTE BUSH

Like many other dune plants, coyote bush has resinous leaves with a strong, pungent odor that should deter herbivores. But insects such as the minute green slug caterpillar have adapted to eating the leaves of coyote bush. Their odd-shaped bodies blend in quite well with the leaves and are hard to detect.

Other moth caterpillars have also made coyote bush their home. On many leaves are tiny teetering brown cases with a small head and the tips of legs protruding at one end. This is the mobile home of the case-bearer caterpillar. Rarely, it can be coaxed out of its case, but never all the way since the occupant takes no chances on being exposed. Additional caterpillars include that of the elegant moth and a leaf roller.

Another well-hidden insect herbivore is a tiny gall gnat whose secretions turn the leaf buds of coyote bush into swollen monstrosities. Within these galls live young maggots that appear to have a perfect life, which includes a surplus of food and protection from enemies. On the stems and leaves of coyote bush live small aphids and two-spotted spider mites. The yellow mites often scurry around so quickly that it's impossible to detect the movement of their eight legs, except when they stop now and then to pierce the leaf surface with their microscopic mouth hooks and suck up some nourishment.

COYOTE BUSH COMMUNITY	
Herbivores	Parasites
Bees	Parasitic wasps
Wasps	Seashore paintbrush
Slug caterpillar	
Case-bearer caterpillar	
Elegant moth	
Leaf-roller caterpillar	
Bud gall gnat	
Aphid	
Two-spotted spider mite	

COYOTE BUSH

(*Baccharis pilularis*: Asteraceae)

Characteristics: Much-branched ever-green shrub with small, thick, resinous, entire or slightly toothed leaves. Small whitish female and male flowers occur on separate plants. Seeds are covered with woolly white hairs for dispersal.

Habitat and range: Dunes in Oregon and California.

Comments: Many herbivorous insects occur on coyote bush in spite of the resin-ous, leathery leaves. Coyote bush is also a source of nectar for a variety of insects, especially bees and wasps.

SLUG CATERPILLAR

(*Oidaematophorus confusus*: Lepidoptera: Pterophoridae)

Characteristics: The small green caterpillar is straight and slug shaped. The head is directed downward and partially withdrawn into the thorax. Fringes of spinelike setae occur on the tips of the body. The adult moth is brown, with long, narrow wings and extended legs.

Habitat and range: Dunes in Oregon and California.

Comments: The flattened caterpillars feed completely exposed during the day and remain motionless unless disturbed, at which time they curl up and drop to the ground. Several parasitic wasps attack the caterpillars.

CASE-BEARER CATERPILLAR

(*Coleophora* sp.: Lepidoptera: Coleophoridae)

Characteristics: The small, light green caterpillars have a dark head and live inside longitudinally grooved brown cases.

Habitat and range: Dunes in California and Oregon.

Comments: The caterpillars carry their elongated cases continuously and add material to them as they grow. Only their head, prothorax, and leg tips are exposed when feeding.

ELEGANT MOTH

(*Aristotelia*: Lepidoptera: Gelechiidae)

Characteristics: Caterpillars are small and brown and mottled with white specks. Adult moths are small and brown, with white and dark markings on the forewings and legs. The wing tips support a cluster of erect brown scales.

Habitat and range: Dunes in Oregon and California.

Comments: Caterpillars live in silken tubes and skeletonize the leaves. The newly hatched caterpillars sometimes begin development in gnat bud galls, which destroys the galls along with the gnat larvae.

LEAF-ROLLER CATERPILLAR

(Lepidoptera: Tortricidae)

Characteristics: Caterpillars small and light green, with a shiny olive-green head capsule.

Habitat and range: Dunes in Oregon and California.

Comments: These caterpillars live within leaves they have bound together with silk. Adult moths were not obtained.

BUD GALL GNAT

(*Rhopalomyia californica*: Diptera: Cecidomyiidae)

Characteristics: Larvae small, pale white, maggot-like. Adult gnats small and dark bodied, with clear, wide wings, long antennae, and extended legs. Red eggs are deposited in clusters on the buds.

Habitat and range: Dunes along the Pacific Northwest coast and elsewhere.

Comments: The light green galls, which are located in the flower heads, can transform the entire head into bulbous, puffy tissue. The pupal skins often remain attached to the outer gall wall after the adults leave. Larvae of a second gall gnat, *Rhopalomyia baccharis*, live in dark brown stem galls on coyote bush.

APHID

(*Aphis* sp.: Hemiptera: Aphididae)

Characteristics: Small, light to dark green aphids covered with short setae and with the basal half of the antennae whitish. Cornicles (tubes on back) dark brown, short, and wide.

Habitat and range: Dunes in Oregon.

Comments: The aphids use coyote bush as a summer host.

TWO-SPOTTED SPIDER MITE

(*Tetranychus bimaculatus*: Acari: Tetranychidae)

Characteristics: Elliptical, soft-bodied, small brownish mite with a large black spot on each side of the body.

Habitat and range: Dunes along the Pacific coast and elsewhere.

Comments: Two-spotted spider mites have an extremely wide host range. They often spin a fine web over their feeding sites, where they pierce the plant surface and imbibe the juices.

SEASHORE PAINTBRUSH

(*Castilleja exserta* subsp. *latifolia*: Scrophulariaceae)

Characteristics: An erect, semiparasitic perennial with red-tipped flowers and oblong, usually entire and finely villous leaves. Stems arise from the base of the host plant.

Habitat and range: Coastal dunes from Washington to Baja California.

Comments: Parasitic members of this genus form suckers that invade the roots of host plants for nourishment. The species is composed of a number of lineages that parasitize different dune plants, including beach wormwood.

GUM PLANT

It's easy to get your fingers covered with sticky white latex when you examine the flower clusters of gum plant. While the purpose of the milky fluid that flows out of cut leaves and collects in the unopened flower buds is a mystery, it does act as a good repellent to any creature considering eating the plant. The latex contains a number of chemicals, including one that makes latex paint freeze resistant and was important enough to warrant a patent.

Feeding among the leaves and stems of gum plants are beautifully camouflaged stubby green weevil larvae. And buried in the sand at the base of the plant are their greenish pupae, which flip over when touched. The molted brown adults are difficult to find since they match the sand grains so well.

The flowers attract a number of insects, including leaf-cutter bees, so named because they are excellent craftsmen capable of cutting out leaf disks of different shapes and sizes to line their nests. Deep in the flowers are striped plume moth caterpillars, while feeding on the petals are flower caterpillars covered with a series of stubby sharp spines.

What a surprise it is to discover a cluster of pink flowers emerging from the base of dune gum plant. There are no stems or leaves attached to this cluster of pink flowers, since the blooms grow directly out of the sand. Removing the sand reveals that the roots of this parasitic broomrape plant are attached to those of the dune gum plant. Broomrape taps into the gum plant for food and is just as much a pest as the little weevil that feeds on the leaves.

Another parasitic plant attacking the gum plant has long, narrow, ropelike stems that wrap around the leaves of its victim. This dodder plant forms small outgrowths from its stems that penetrate the tissues of the gum plant for nourishment. The tiny white dodder flowers are quite attractive and innocent looking, concealing the plant's parasitic nature.

GUM PLANT COMMUNITY	
Herbivores	Parasites
Wasp	Wasp
Weevil	Broomrape
Plume moth	Dodder
Leaf-cutter bee	
Flower caterpillar	

GUM PLANT

(*Grindelia integrifolia*: Asteraceae)

Characteristics: Perennial with thick, entire or slightly toothed leaves. Large yellow flowers with numerous long, slender ray petals. Leaves exude latex when broken. Flower buds covered with a sticky deposit, giving the plant its common name.

Habitat and range: Dunes from Washington to California.

Comments: The plants prefer damp habitats in low areas (deflation plains) of the dunes. Leaf-cutter bees and wasps visit the flowers.

WEEVIL

(*Listroderes* sp.: Coleoptera: Curculionidae)

Characteristics: Larva legless, shiny, light green with a tan head capsule. Pupa light green, formed in soil. Adult pale brown, wing covers with dark and light spotting and a distinct white accent mark near the tip.

Habitat and range: Dunes in California.

Comments: The larvae feed on the leaves at night and hide in the sand during the day.

PLUME MOTH

(*Platyptilia* sp.: Lepidoptera: Pterophoridae)

Characteristics: Caterpillar small, pale, with red bands running the length of the body. Adult moth slender, midsized, with long legs and narrow, light gray wings with darker markings near the tip.

Habitat and range: Dunes from Washington to California.

Comments: The larvae are deeply embedded in the flower heads and feed on the developing seeds.

LEAF-CUTTER BEE

(*Megachile* sp.: Hymenoptera: Megachilidae)

Characteristics: A midsized, hairy black bee with clear wings and a series of white stripes across the abdomen.

Habitat and range: Dunes from Washington to California and elsewhere.

Comments: Leaf-cutter bees visit several dune flowers for pollen and nectar besides those of gum plant. The females are adept at cutting out sections of leaves for nest material.

FLOWER CATERPILLAR

(*Heliothis* sp.: Lepidoptera)

Characteristics: Large, pale green caterpillar with abdominal segments bearing stubby spines, each capped with a fine hair. A dark stripe runs the length of the body on each side. Pupa dark orange, formed in soil.

Habitat and range: Dunes in Oregon.

Comments: A parasitic wasp develops inside the caterpillars, and when mature, the wasp larva drops to the ground and spins a tightly woven silken cocoon for pupation. Adult moths were not obtained.

BROOMRAPE

(*Orobanche californica* subsp. *californica*: Orobanchaceae)

Characteristics: Plant without leaves or a noticeable stem. Flowers spreading, pink with lavender veins.

Habitat and range: Dunes from British Columbia to California.

Comments: This gum plant parasite gives the impression that the flowers emerge directly from the soil.

DODDER

(*Cuscuta* sp.: Cuscutaceae)

Characteristics: Parasitic plants lacking chlorophyll, with wiry yellow stems that twine around the host plant. The leaves are reduced to small scales and the flowers are minute white cups with protruding stamens.

Habitat and range: Dunes and wet areas from Washington to California.

Comments: After dodder becomes firmly established with a host plant, its root system dies and all nutrients are obtained from its victim. Dodder strangles its host by producing outgrowths (haustoria) that enter the tissues and remove nutrients. Other dune plants are also victims of this parasite. Viruses can be transmitted from infected to healthy plants by a bridging dodder parasitizing both.

RAGWORT

Several types of ragwort plants occur along the Pacific coastal dunes. Two introduced species are tansy ragwort and cutleaf ragwort, while the rare sand dune ragwort is a native of California. Unfortunately, the latter grows only along the central California coast and may soon become extinct. All three species have yellow flowers and long blooming periods, usually extending from late spring into fall.

One ragwort that prevails throughout the Pacific Northwest is tansy ragwort, which finds the stabilized dunes to its liking. Unfortunately, it is toxic to livestock, especially horses and cows. Even milk can contain the poisonous alkaloids, as can honey made from bees visiting the flowers. As a result, the Department of Agriculture authorized the importation of several Old World insect herbivores. One of these is the beautiful cinnabar moth, whose striking caterpillars can be found on tansy ragwort in late spring and early summer. The immature caterpillars are covered with black spots, and the older ones have black stripes against an orange background. One would think that the contrasting colors would attract predators, but these aposematic colors warn predators that the caterpillars contain toxic compounds and are unpalatable. Along with the cinnabar moths, a seed-head maggot and a flea beetle were also imported from Europe for biological control of tansy ragwort. All three of these insect herbivores are now well established along the Pacific Northwest coast.

Cutleaf ragwort, bearing very short petals and lobed leaves, can be found in remote dune areas. However, it doesn't take long for aphids to detect the plants, and they quickly proliferate before their food source disappears in the next storm. The shrub-like sand dune ragwort, unlike the other ragworts, has extremely slender leaves and a hardy root system.

RAGWORT COMMUNITY
Herbivores
Cinnabar moth
Seed-head maggot
Flea beetle
Aphid

TANSY RAGWORT

(*Senecio jacobaea*: Asteraceae)

Characteristic: A short-lived perennial with long solitary stems that are twice to many times divided and have terminal clusters of yellow flowers. The leaves are narrow and pinnately lobed, and the flowers contain both long ray and short disk florets. The flowering period is from June to September.

Habitat and range: Pacific Northwest and other areas in North America.

Comments: This plant, which is native to Eurasia, has alkaloids that are poisonous to horses and cattle. The insects mentioned here have all been introduced from Eurasia for biological control of tansy ragwort.

CUTLEAF RAGWORT

(*Senecio glomeratus*: Asteraceae)

Characteristic: A tall annual or short-lived perennial with numerous branching flower stems bearing many yellow disk florets and a few short yellow ray florets. Leaves are broad, small, and pinnately lobed.

Habitat and range: Pacific Northwest from Washington to California.

Comments: This species is native to Australia and New Zealand. The flowering period is from April to September. It can appear anywhere on the dunes, and many of the plants are attacked by aphids.

SAND DUNE RAGWORT

(*Senecio blochmaniae*: Asteraceae)

Characteristic: A perennial subshrub with a woody taproot and yellow ray and disk florets. Leaves fleshy, linear to threadlike, crowded on stems.

Habitat and range: Endemic to the central coast of California.

Comments: The blooming period of this rare species, also known as Blochman's ragwort, is from May to November.

CINNABAR MOTH

(*Tyria jacobaeae*: Lepidoptera: Arctiidae)
Characteristics: Immature caterpillars are orange with black spots. Mature caterpillars are large and orange, with black bands encircling each segment. The pupae are tan at first and then darken to reddish brown. The large adults have bluish-gray forewings, each with a red bar along the outer edge and two terminal red spots. The hind wings are completely red.
Habitat and range: Throughout the Pacific Northwest.
Comments: The cinnabar moth is native to Eurasia and was imported from France into California in 1959 for biological control of tansy ragwort. Both the caterpillars and adults have warning (aposematic) colors indicating that they contain toxic alkaloids.

SEED-HEAD MAGGOT

(*Botanophila seneciella*: Diptera: Anthomyiidae)
Characteristics: Maggots small, robust, white, with black mouth hooks. Puparia dark brown. Adult flies small, resembling houseflies, but with red eyes.
Habitat and range: In coastal and other habitats throughout the Pacific Northwest.
Comments: The seed-head maggot was imported from France into California in 1966 for biological control of tansy ragwort. The maggots develop in the flower receptacles and feed on the developing seeds. They produce a frothy spittle from their anus that emerges from the top of infested flowers.

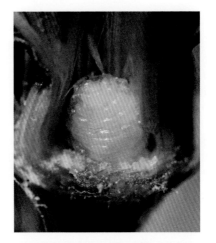

FLEA BEETLE

(*Longitarsus jacobaeae*: Coleoptera: Chrysomelidae)
Characteristics: A very small tan beetle with long antennae and powerful hind legs adapted for jumping.
Habitat and range: In coastal and other habitats throughout the Pacific Northwest.
Comments: This flea beetle was imported from Italy and Switzerland into California in 1969 for biological control of tansy ragwort. The larvae feed on the roots and the adults feed on the leaves.

PACIFIC SILVERWEED

The delicate yellow flowers of Pacific silverweed are common along most of the Pacific coast, especially in damp marshy areas and sandy shores where sand is mixed with organic matter. The spreading runners crawl over anything in their path, including fallen logs, and can intertwine, forming a tight network that can trip a person. The leaflets are delicately incised along the edges and silvery beneath, giving the plant its common name.

Various flies and bees visit the flowers for pollen and nectar. One unusual visitor is a forest yellow jacket whose yellow bands match the color of the petals. Forest yellow jackets are not common among the open sand dunes and spend most of their time in adjacent dune forests. Since they collect only living arthropods to feed their young, they don't pester humans, unlike the common yellow jackets that come to our picnic tables.

Herbivores are not common on Pacific silverweed, and the little caterpillars I discovered all reside in folded leaflets, making them difficult to see. One is almost completely black, and the other is pale green with a tan head. The pupae of both moths are formed within the leaflets and share a similar brown color, but the adult moths have quite different hues.

An amazing wasp parasitizes the green caterpillars. The wasp lays eggs that divide into several embryos inside the parasitized caterpillar. This condition, called polyembryony, makes it possible for the wasp to produce numerous offspring from a single egg. In the end, the dying caterpillar is filled with numerous wasp pupae that synchronously produce many small adults.

Chewing away on the leaf surfaces are black flea beetles. The larvae have a wrinkled appearance, as if they were wearing a suit too large for them. The adult beetles, on the other hand, are smooth and shiny.

PACIFIC SILVERWEED COMMUNITY	
Herbivores	Parasites
Flies	Wasps
Bees	
Forest yellow jacket	
Black leaf caterpillar	
Green leaf caterpillar	
Flea beetle	

PACIFIC SILVERWEED

(*Potentilla anserina* subsp. *pacifica*: Rosaceae)

Characteristics: Low perennial spreading by runners (stolons). Leaves smooth, pinnately compound, white or silvery and hairy beneath. Flowers yellow, positioned at the tips of solitary naked stems arising from the runners.

Habitat and range: Dunes and open marshy areas from Alaska to California and elsewhere.

Comments: The plants spread by long runners that can form networks covering driftwood and entire dune areas. They flower from May through summer and into fall.

FOREST YELLOW JACKET

(*Vespula acadica*: Hymenoptera: Vespidae)

Characteristics: Short, midsized black wasp with a few yellow markings on the thorax, and yellow bands and two separate yellow spots on the abdomen.

Habitat and range: Widespread from Alaska to California.

Comments: Forest yellow jackets visit numerous flowers besides those of Pacific silverweed for nectar and pollen. They collect living arthropods as food for their larvae and are not scavengers.

BLACK LEAF CATERPILLAR

(*Olethreutes cespitana*: Lepidoptera: Tortricidae)

Characteristics: Caterpillars black to dark brown. Pupae dark brown. Adults small, with dark brown forewings crossed by two irregular light bands.

Habitat and range: Western North America.

Comments: This moth has a wide host range, especially members of the Rosaceae family. The dark color of the caterpillar is unusual since leaf caterpillars are usually green or tan.

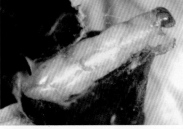

GREEN LEAF CATERPILLAR

(*Acleris* sp.: Lepidoptera: Tortricidae)

Characteristics: Green caterpillar with a tan head. Pupa dark brown. Adult midsized, uniformly rusty brown.

Habitat and range: Dunes in Oregon.

Comments: The caterpillars are usually well hidden within curled leaves but are parasitized by wasps (*Litomastix* sp.: Hymenoptera: Encyrtidae). The eggs of the wasp divide inside the caterpillar (polyembryony), which explains the large number of small wasps that emerge from the dead host.

FLEA BEETLE

(*Altica* sp.: Coleoptera: Chrysomelidae)

Characteristics: Larvae small, short, black, with wrinkly skin folds. Adults small, metallic bronze, shiny, capable of jumping with their thick hind legs.

Habitat and range: Dunes from Washington to California.

Comments: The larvae feed only on the surface of the leaves, thus exposing the lighter underlying tissues.

COAST WILLOW

Coast willows are pioneers in that they invade the foredunes and can withstand having their roots inundated with each high tide. In this setting they have no other tree competitors in the Pacific Northwest, and their abundance, rapid growth, and durability make them ideal plants for herbivores. They can be considered a keystone species since so many organisms are dependent on them. As early as March, or even earlier in some years, the fluffy light green catkins, or flower spikes, appear on the upright branches, usually while the leaves are still in bud.

The male catkins are visited by bees and flies, especially the early-to-appear orange-rumped bumblebees. One little brown weevil utilizes the male flowers as a food source. Willow catkins are a rare developmental site for insects because they are formed early in the spring when the weather is still cold, last only a few days, and then wither away and drop after shedding their pollen. But pollen is an excellent source of protein and, together with the adjacent long, silken hairs, makes a perfect home for the willow catkin weevil. The eggs are laid at the base of the tiny flowers, and the legless white larvae soon eat out a little lair among the hairs. When the catkins drop, the mature larvae leave and pupate in the sand. Aside from a few parasitic mites, no other herbivores or carnivores were found to share this habitat with these weevils.

Of all the insect herbivores on coast willow, the little sawfly that forms red leaf galls is one of my favorites. These galls resemble cherries or little red apples and are initiated when the female sawfly places an egg in the leaf tissue. This stimulates the growth of surrounding plant cells so that by the time the egg hatches, the larva is enclosed in a domicile. But this is a home where the surrounding walls keep growing inward as well as outward, so the sawfly larva must keep feeding or it can become immobilized by the same elements that are nourishing it. Several opened galls revealed larvae that suffered that fate. When mature, the larva eats a hole in the side, emerges, falls to the ground, and forms a cocoon that eventually produces an adult.

However, life is not all nice and cozy for the sawfly. Other insects depend on these sawflies for their own existence, and still others are opportunists that step in to take advantage of the situation. Parasitic wasps search out the galls and insert their own eggs into the tissue. Their larvae then dispatch those of the sawfly. A metallic beetle enters the galls to feed on the occupants. Moths lay their eggs next to the galls and the caterpillars devour the sawfly larvae along with the gall tissue. The complexities of life surrounding these red leaf galls is amazing and could fill the pages of a book. A number of insects feed on the leaves of coast willow. These include leaf beetles, sawfly larvae, moth caterpillars, and aphids, all of which have their own life dramas.

COAST WILLOW COMMUNITY	
Herbivores	Parasites/Predators/Symbionts
Orange-rumped bumblebee	Red leaf gall wasps
Willow leaf beetle	Aphid wasp
Spotted willow leaf beetle	Willow catkin weevil mites
Bold leaf beetle	Soft-winged flower beetle
Red-headed leaf caterpillar	Dune ants
Willow green stem gall fly	Ladybird beetles
Red leaf gall sawfly	Bald-faced hornets
Red leaf gall caterpillar	
Willow catkin weevil	
Black-spotted willow sawfly	
Spotted tussock moth	
Green willow sawfly	
Red willow aphid	
Willow flea beetle	

COAST WILLOW

(*Salix hookeriana*: Salicaceae)

Characteristics: Shrub to small tree with oval to lanceolate deciduous leaves that are white hairy beneath. Flowers arranged in male and female catkins that appear in the spring before the leaves emerge.

Habitat and range: Dunes from Alaska to California.

Comments: Coast willow supplies food for numerous insects. It survives by outgrowing its attackers. One of the common pollinators on the catkins is the orange-rumped bumblebee (*Bombus melanopygus*: Hymenoptera: Apidae).

WILLOW LEAF BEETLE

(*Galerucella decora*: Coleoptera: Chrysomelidae)

Characteristics: Larva yellow and covered with black tubercles and stripes. Adult small, oblong, brownish yellow, with darker regions along edges of the wing covers. Pronotum wide, bearing three dark spots.

Habitat and range: Dunes from Washington to California and elsewhere.

Comments: The larvae usually feed only on the upper surface of the leaves. They also attack other types of willow.

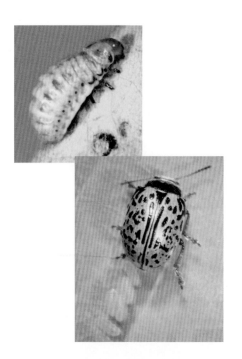

SPOTTED WILLOW LEAF BEETLE

(*Calligrapha multipunctata*: Coleoptera: Chrysomelidae)

Characteristics: Larvae cream colored, with faint dark markings on body segments and a tan head. Adult large, with a black pronotum and yellow wing covers bearing black dots and dashes. Eggs oblong, bright yellow.

Habitat and range: Dunes from British Columbia to California.

Comments: These beetles can build up large numbers in the spring.

BOLD LEAF BEETLE

(*Chrysomela aeneicollis*: Coleoptera: Chrysomelidae)

Characteristics: Adults small, with a black head and thorax and orange wing covers mottled with dark patterns.

Habitat and range: Widespread in North America.

Comments: This beetle has many color variations and feeds on a variety of willows.

RED-HEADED LEAF CATERPILLAR

(*Phlogophora* sp.: Lepidoptera: Noctuidae)

Characteristics: Large, stout caterpillar with a shiny red head and tan body bearing minute white spots.

Habitat and range: Dunes in Oregon.

Comments: The red head is very characteristic, but other color variants also occur.

WILLOW GREEN STEM GALL FLY

(*Dasineura* sp.: Diptera: Cecidomyiidae)

Characteristics: Larvae minute, elongated, legless, reddish yellow. Adults small and gray, with long legs and short antennae.

Habitat and range: Dunes from Washington to California.

Comments: The green galls are located on the stems. Multiple larvae can occur in the same gall. A sawfly (*Euura* sp.: Hymenoptera: Tenthredinidae) also forms galls on the stems and leaf petioles of coast willow.

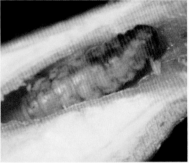

RED LEAF GALL SAWFLY
(*Pontania* sp.: Hymenoptera: Tenthredinidae)

Characteristics: Larvae small, white with a brown head, living in large cherry-sized galls on leaves. Adult sawflies small, black, with transparent wings and a broad head. **Habitat and range:** Dunes from Washington to California and elsewhere. **Comments:** Wasps in the genera *Bracon* (Hymenoptera: Braconidae) and *Pteromalus* (Hymenoptera: Chalcididae) parasitize the larvae inside the galls. A soft-winged flower beetle (*Collops*: Coleoptera: Malachidae) moves from gall to gall, opening them and devouring the sawfly larvae. A small, rectangular brown moth (*Acleris* sp.: Lepidoptera: Tortricidae, middle left) lays eggs on the galls, and the hatching caterpillars, which are brown with two white dorsal stripes, enter the galls, destroy the sawfly larvae, and then feed on the gall tissue. A second small caterpillar does the same.

WILLOW CATKIN WEEVIL

(*Dorytomus* sp.: Coleoptera: Curculionidae)

Characteristics: Larva small, white, greatly curved, legless, with a brown head. Adult small, reddish brown, with a long, slender beak.

Habitat and range: Dunes from Washington to California.

Comments: The eggs and larvae occur in the catkins. The pupae are formed in small depressions in the sand.

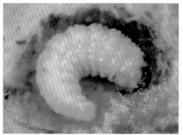

BLACK-SPOTTED WILLOW SAWFLY

(*Nematus chalceus*: Hymenoptera: Tenthredinidae)

Characteristics: Larvae green to yellow, becoming large, with back and sides covered with black spots and dashes. Cocoons brown, fibrous, egg shaped to elliptical. Adults large, with a black head and a dark brown to black body with transparent wings.

Habitat and range: Dunes in Washington and Oregon.

Comments: The larvae often feed in groups and, when disturbed, raise their tails and emit a liquid that supposedly deters enemies. That does not protect them from small parasitic wasps (bottom right).

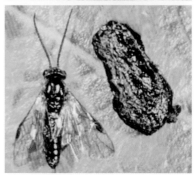

SPOTTED TUSSOCK MOTH

(*Lophocampa maculata*: Lepidoptera: Arctiidae)

Characteristics: Young caterpillar white, with long white body hairs and a row of red setal clusters on the back. Mature caterpillar large, black, with an orange-brown midsection and protruding tufts of long white hairs. Adult moth very large, yellowish tan, with darker markings across the forewings.

Habitat and range: Widespread throughout western North America.

Comments: The color patterns of the caterpillars vary with age and host plant. They are usually found on willow leaves in the fall. The dark brown pupa, together with the last shed skin of the caterpillar, occurs within the cocoon.

RED WILLOW APHID

(*Uroleucon* sp.: Hemiptera: Aphididae)

Characteristics: Abdomen brown and head and prothorax orange-red. Antennae long, darkening toward tips. Winged adult greenish, with dark bands across the abdomen.

Habitat and Range: Dunes in Oregon and California.

Comments: Dune ants and bald-faced hornets obtain honeydew from the aphids while ladybird beetles prey on the aphids.

BALD-FACED HORNET

(*Dolichovespula maculata*: Hymenoptera: Vespidae)

Characteristics: Large black and white wasps with a white "bald" head and three white bands at the tip of the abdomen.

Habitat and Range: Widespread throughout most of North America.

Comments: The workers are carnivores but will also take nectar from flowers and honeydew from aphids. Numerous insects and other types of arthropods are fed to the developing young. Bald-faced hornets make oval paper nests from masticated wood fibers. They guard their nests and are quick to attack and sting anyone that approaches too closely.

GORSE

In England, gorse is planted as hedgerows because it provides a living fence that no animal can traverse. This is because the leaflets develop into large, sharp spines that function like barbed wire. Although the yellow flowers are attractive, it is surprising that it was introduced as an ornamental and sand stabilizer in spite of its painful defensive features.

Gorse was eventually found to be more of a pest than a benefit since it rapidly spreads out of control and the seeds can remain viable for over twenty years. Biological agents were imported from Europe to help keep gorse under control. Along the dunes, a European seed weevil appears to be the only biological control agent that survives in the coastal climate. It is strange to see the minute adults resting on the large, treacherous spines.

Gorse Community
Herbivores
Gorse seed weevil
Red gorse spider mite

GORSE
(*Ulex europaeus*: Fabaceae)
Characteristics: Shrub with large, yellow, pealike flowers and spine-covered stems. Seedlings have alternate leaves composed of three narrow leaflets that later become spines. Fruit a hairy, flattened black pod. Blooms from spring to autumn.
Habitat and range: Dunes and inland from British Columbia to California.
Comments: This noxious plant was imported from Scotland in the late 1800s as an ornamental and hedge plant. It spread and now crowds out native vegetation and forms impenetrable thickets that become fire hazards during dry periods. The gorse seed weevil and red gorse spider mite (*Tetranychus lintearius*) were imported as biological control agents of gorse. The mites live in webbed colonies and imbibe plant juices. Only seed weevils were found in coastal habitats.

DUNE PLANT COMMUNITIES: GORSE

GORSE SEED WEEVIL

(*Exapion ulicis*: Coleoptera: Brentidae)

Characteristics: Small, long-snouted weevil covered with white scales, except for the black beak and antennae. Larvae white, curved, legless.

Habitat and range: Throughout the range of gorse from British Columbia to California.

Comments: The gorse seed weevil was imported from France into California in 1953 for biological control of gorse. The larvae consume the developing seeds within the pods and the adults feed on the stems and spines.

SEASIDE TANSY

The round yellow flowers, finely dissected leaves, and odor readily identify seaside tansy. The camphor and other compounds in the leaves not only produce a strong, pungent smell but can also cause a dermatitis that may form blisters.

These annoying chemicals, which may function as effective insecticides, are more concentrated in the leaves than in the flowers, which explains why all the insect herbivores I saw on this plant were attacking the flowers. Plume moth caterpillars share the flowers with white flower fly maggots. Small wasps deposit their eggs in the developing maggots, but the wasp larvae don't start feeding until the maggots have finished their development and have pupated. So the wasp larvae end up with a secure home filled with food. An opened parasitized puparium shows that the wasp has eaten all traces of its victim, leaving its home clean and empty.

SEASIDE TANSY COMMUNITY	
Herbivores	Parasites
Seaside tansy plume moth	Wasp
Seaside tansy flower fly	

SEASIDE TANSY
(*Tanacetum bipinnatum*: Asteraceae)
Characteristics: Yellow-flowered perennial with finely dissected, elongated leaves and spreading roots (rhizomes). The leaves are two to three times divided and bear some white-woolly hairs. Crushed leaves smell strongly of camphor.
Habitat and range: Dunes from British Columbia to California and elsewhere.
Comments: Compounds in the leaves can cause dermatitis.

SEASIDE TANSY PLUME MOTH

(*Oidaematophorus* sp.: Lepidoptera:
Pterophoridae)

Characteristics: Caterpillar pale cream,
with a black head and three red lines running the length of the body. Adult large
and slender, with long, narrow, mottled
brown wings.

Habitat and range: Dunes in Oregon and
California.

Comments: The caterpillars burrow into
the base of the flower heads.

SEASIDE TANSY FLOWER FLY

(*Tephritis candidipennis*: Diptera:
Tephritidae)

Characteristics: Small grayish fly with
large iridescent eyes and membranous
wings with dark markings. Maggots white,
legless.

Habitat and range: Dunes in Oregon and
California.

Comments: The larva, which burrows
into the flower heads, is parasitized by
a small wasp that devours it and then
pupates within the victim's puparium
(bottom right).

YARROW

The white, or occasionally yellow or pink, flower clusters of yarrow are on display all summer along the dunes as well as inland. Yarrow is quite adaptable: the coastal forms are a bit smaller, probably as a result of the constant winds, than those growing inland. The entire plant is very aromatic and has been used for its analgesic, antimicrobial, and decongestant properties.

A lot of activity occurs on the flower heads of yarrow, perhaps because the aromatic compounds are less abundant there than in the leaves. Velvet longhorn beetles visit the blooms and are fairly easy to catch when so occupied. Flies and bees also probe the flowers for nectar and pollen. However, flower flies may be in for a surprise when they choose a flower cluster in which a crab spider happens to be resting. White crab spiders blend in perfectly with the yarrow flowers and are very patient, waiting motionless for hours for a visiting insect. Once a victim is caught, there is little chance of escape, and it is quickly sucked dry and then dropped to the ground. Unopened flower heads provide an ideal resting spot for harvestmen, which engulf the entire bud surface with their long legs.

The red-striped plume moth caterpillar prefers to eat the flowers but, if food is scarce, will eat its way through the flower stems as well. When finished feeding, the caterpillar forms a slender pupa between the florets. From this pupa emerges a very slender moth with extremely long legs and amazingly narrow wings that are often held outstretched like those of an aircraft glider when resting.

Feeding on the surface of the stems are looper or inchworm caterpillars that move by a series of loops as they "inch" along the stems. They appear to avoid the leaves as a source of nourishment, and some caterpillars prefer to reside in the roots and pupate in the soil. After emerging, mottled-brown root moths often rest motionless on the flower heads.

YARROW COMMUNITY	
Herbivores	Predators
Velvet long-horned beetle	Crab spider
Flower fly	Harvestman
Mason bee	
Red-striped plume moth	
Looper	
Root moth	

YARROW

(*Achillea millefolium*: Asteraceae)

Characteristics: Perennial herb with finely dissected aromatic leaves and multiple clusters of white flowers borne at the tips of stems. Some varieties have pink or yellow flowers.

Habitat and range: Dunes from Washington to California and other areas in North America.

Comments: The coastal forms are shorter than the inland varieties. Yarrow is fairly resistant to insects and disease, possibly because of its aromatic compounds. Flowers appear in late summer and fall and attract beetles, flies, spiders, and harvestmen.

VELVET LONG-HORNED BEETLE

(*Cosmosalia chrysocoma*: Coleoptera: Cerambycidae)

Characteristics: Large, dark brown beetle with a wedge-shaped body, large protruding eyes, and long antennae. The thorax and wing covers are covered with short golden hairs.

Habitat and range: Dunes from Washington to California and elsewhere.

Comments: The adults, which may have a yellowish sheen, feed on flowers for pollen and nectar and may serve as pollinators. The larvae develop in living and dying wood.

CRAB SPIDER

(*Misumena* sp.: Araneae: Thomisidae)

Characteristics: Small, white to yellow spiders with the first two pairs of legs elongated. Crab spiders have the habit of holding their front legs out and curved inward like crabs as they await their prey on flowers. They can also move quickly sideways and backward like a crab.

Habitat and range: Dunes from Washington to California.

Comments: Crab spiders usually choose flowers that match their color, remaining motionless as they wait for pollinators to arrive. Flower flies (Diptera: Syrphidae) are frequent victims.

MASON BEE

(*Anthidium* sp.: Hymenoptera: Megachilidae)

Characteristics: A midsized black bee with a series of short yellow bands on each side of the abdomen.

Habitat and range: Dunes from Washington to California and elsewhere.

Comments: Mason bees are solitary and visit many flowers for nectar and pollen. They carry pollen in hairs on the underside of their abdomen.

HARVESTMAN

(*Phalangium opilio*: Opiliones: Phalangiidae)

Characteristics: Short, roundish, brown body with a small head and very long legs. An irregular, wide, dark brown band extends the length of the abdomen.

Habitat and range: This introduced species occurs in various habitats, including coastal dunes, around the world.

Comments: Harvestmen, or daddy longlegs, do not construct webs and often wait on plants for insect prey to appear.

RED-STRIPED PLUME MOTH

(*Gillmeria pallidactyla*: Lepidoptera: Pterophoridae)

Characteristics: Caterpillars yellow to white, with several dark reddish bands running the length of the body. The adult moths are extremely slender, with narrow wings slightly expanded at the tip, and long legs.

Habitat and range: Dunes from Washington to California and elsewhere in North America.

Comments: Holding the narrow wings outstretched is typical for many plume moths. The caterpillars first feed around the flower bases and then burrow into the flower stems. This can result in retarded plant growth and a "bunched" condition of the terminal leaves and flower heads.

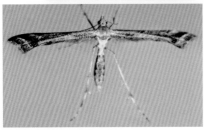

LOOPER

(Lepidoptera: Geometridae)

Characteristics: Large, light gray caterpillar with a brown head. The true legs are positioned near the head and the prolegs occur at the tail. This leg arrangement restricts walking to a looping motion.

Habitat and range: Dunes in Oregon and California.

Comments: The caterpillars "freeze" when detected and look like broken stems. Adults were not obtained.

ROOT MOTH

(*Pelochrista* sp.: Lepidoptera: Tortricidae)

Characteristics: Adult moths small, with mottled brown wings. Caterpillars white, develop in the roots of yarrow.

Habitat and range: Dunes in California and Oregon.

Comments: This moth is one of a small group whose caterpillars feed on plant roots.

FIREWEED

Fireweed occurs throughout the Northern Hemisphere, and populations along the Pacific coast show that the plant can tolerate a certain amount of salt spray. The large, attractive, pink to red flowers of fireweed stand out boldly against the dark green leaves.

The short, stocky larvae of fireweed gall gnats develop between folded or curled leaves. The damage they cause while feeding is hardly noticeable, and their only protection is the leaf surface and a self-made silken safety net to keep them from falling. This safety net is later reinforced and made into a thick cocoon where a pupa is formed, which eventually transforms into a long-legged, flimsy adult.

FIREWEED COMMUNITY
Herbivores
Gall gnat

FIREWEED
(*Chamerion angustifolium*: Onagraceae)
Characteristics: Fast-growing, tall peren-nial herb with straight, often reddish stems; entire, narrow, alternate leaves; and deep pink flowers borne in spikes at the tops of the stems. The seeds are equipped with silky hairs for wind dispersal.
Habitat and range: Dunes along the Pacific Northwest coast and elsewhere.
Comments: An unusual leaf feature is that the tips of the veins curl around to meet the adjoining vein instead of continuing to the edge of the leaf.

FIREWEED GALL GNAT
(*Contarinia* sp.: Diptera: Cecidomyiidae)
Characteristics: Larva small, yellowish orange, and slug shaped. The head contains a pair of mouth hooks. The small adult fly is brown and spindly, with membranous wings and long legs.
Habitat and range: Dunes in Oregon and California.
Comments: The larvae develop within folded or curled leaves. When mature, they spin a silky cocoon in the same location.

BULL THISTLE

The beautiful, fuzzy pink flowers of bull thistle mask the treacherous spines that lie beneath. Butterflies, bumblebees, and other insects, including bruchid beetles, love the nectar and pollen of bull thistle and can easily avoid its armature, but wildlife and livestock can be injured. Bull thistle is host to some native insects as well as others that were imported to attack different types of exotic thistles. The plume moth, seed-head fly, and seed-head weevil are found on bull thistle along the coast, but whether they are effective control agents is unknown.

BULL THISTLE COMMUNITY	
Herbivores	Parasites
Plume moth	Tachinid fly
Seed-head weevil	
Seed-head fly	
Flower bruchid	
Bumblebees	

BULL THISTLE
(*Cirsium vulgare*: Asteraceae)
Characteristics: Stout biennial with pinkish-purple flowers subtended by spine-tipped bracts, spiny dissected leaves, and spiny winged stems.
Habitat and range: Grassy areas of the back dunes along the Pacific Northwest coast.
Comments: Bull thistle was originally introduced from Eurasia and is now cosmopolitan. Several types of flower flies and bumblebees visit the flowers.

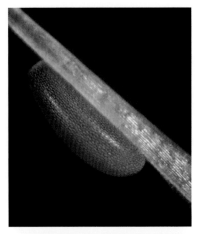

PLUME MOTH

(*Platyptilia* sp.: Lepidoptera: Pterophoridae)

Characteristics: Eggs elongated, with a finely reticulate surface. Caterpillars light green, with longitudinal rows of black spots on the back. Adult moths large, pale brown, slender, with long legs and antennae and narrow wings with dark markings.

Habitat and range: This genus occurs throughout North America.

Comments: The caterpillars are parasitized by tachinid flies that form their sausage-shaped puparia adjacent to the dying host (middle left).

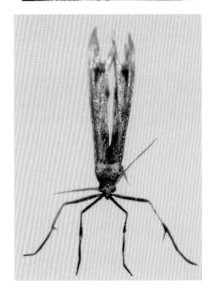

SEED-HEAD WEEVIL

(*Rhinocyllus conicus*: Coleoptera: Curculionidae)

Characteristics: Larva curved, white with a tan head, legless. Adult small, dark brown to black, with a short snout and light spots on the wing covers (elytra).

Habitat and range: Widespread throughout North America.

Comments: This weevil was introduced from Europe for biological control of musk thistle and has spread to other thistles, including some native species. The larvae eat the developing seeds and the adults feed on the flower parts.

SEED-HEAD FLY

(*Urophora stylata*: Diptera: Tephritidae)

Characteristics: The legless white maggots are short and plump. The adult flies are small and brown and have spotted wings. Eggs are deposited in closed flower buds.

Habitat and range: Widespread in North America, Europe, and Asia.

Comments: The larvae are surrounded by gall tissue while developing in the flower buds. This fly was introduced from Europe into North America as a biological control agent of bull thistle but attacks other thistles in the genera *Cirsium* and *Carduus*.

FLOWER BRUCHID

(*Bruchus brachialis*: Coleoptera: Chrysomelidae)

Characteristics: Small, oval black beetle with white scales on the back. Antennae with slender orange basal segments and a broad orange terminal segment.

Habitat and range: Dunes throughout the Pacific Northwest.

Comments: Adult bruchids visit various flowers, including those of bull thistle, for pollen and nectar, and the larvae develop in the seeds of legumes. The larvae of this particular flower bruchid develop in the seeds of vetches.

COAST GOLDENROD

Goldenrods are confined mainly to eastern North America, with a few species in Mexico, South America, Europe, and Asia. The relatively few western species, including coast goldenrod along the Pacific coast, are not well known. The blooms attract a variety of nectar and pollen seekers, including leaf-cutter bees and flower flies. Some insects have adjusted quite well to the resins and terpenes in the tissues of goldenrod, and the allergenic compounds that bother humans don't appear to affect them.

When I examined what appeared to be a trembling leaf on a coast goldenrod stem, I found a small caterpillar concealed inside a well-disguised case. Although carrying around its home would appear to be quite an encumbrance, such a behavior definitely has survival value. When danger threatens, the caterpillar pulls its sturdy case over itself, forming an impenetrable enclosure. The inchworm caterpillar uses a different method of avoiding enemies. Its color resembles that of faded flowers, and when frozen in position, it resembles a broken twig. The flower moth caterpillar has no protective coloration or case, but it rarely exposes itself and remains deeply buried within the flowers. Plume moth caterpillars do this as well, but they do emerge from the flower clusters occasionally, and I can't imagine that the orange stripes along their backs provide that much cover.

The camouflage technique of the adult green leaf beetle is obviously being a color that matches the leaves and stems of coast goldenrod. But the black larvae stand out boldly on the foliage and must have a different strategy for avoiding enemies. The dark larvae of the leaf-mining beetle are able to burrow through the leaf tissue, thus being protected by the leaf surfaces as they feed. The key to survival for red aphids is their small size and rapid reproductive rate.

COAST GOLDENROD COMMUNITY
Herbivores
Leaf-cutter bee
Flower fly
Goldenrod case moth caterpillar
Goldenrod inchworm
Flower moth
Plume moth
Green leaf beetle
Leaf-mining beetle
Red aphid

COAST GOLDENROD

(*Solidago spathulata*: Asteraceae)

Characteristics: Spreading to erect perennial with thick, nearly sessile, resinous leaves; basal leaves spoon shaped; upper leaves linear. Flowers yellow, borne in pyramid-shaped clusters at stem tips.

Habitat and range: Dunes in Oregon and California.

Comments: The height of the plants varies, with the smaller specimens nearer the coastline.

LEAF-CUTTER BEE

(*Dianthidium* sp.: Hymenoptera: Megachilidae)

Characteristics: Slender, small, solitary bee with a grayish head and thorax and a black abdomen with transverse white bands. Wings membranous, mostly clear.

Habitat and range: Dunes from Washington to California and elsewhere.

Comments: This is one of many bees that visit coast goldenrod for pollen and nectar.

FLOWER FLY

(*Syrphus* sp.: Diptera: Syrphidae)

Characteristics: Stout-bodied, large black fly with transverse yellow bands on the abdomen.

Habitat and range: Dunes in Oregon and California.

Comments: There are many flower flies with similar color patters that visit coast goldenrod. Flower flies eat pollen and nectar and the larvae are carnivorous, preying especially on aphids.

GOLDENROD CASE MOTH

(*Coleophora* sp.: Lepidoptera: Coleophoridae)

Characteristics: Larva small, greenish brown, with a brown head and brown spots on the thorax. Larval case tan, surface often adorned with plant hairs and debris.

Habitat and range: Dunes from Washington to California.

Comments: Pupation occurs within the case after it is secured to the plant surface.

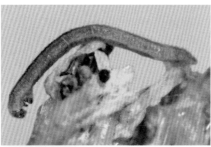

GOLDENROD INCHWORM

(*Eupithecia* sp.: Lepidoptera: Geometridae)

Characteristics: Caterpillar large, grayish brown, long and narrow, with legs at head and tail end only. Adult moth large, grayish brown, with forewings bearing dark spots along the margins and a single spot near the center.

Habitat and range: Dunes in Oregon and California.

Comments: The caterpillars often feed in the flower heads.

FLOWER MOTH

(*Phaneta* sp.: Lepidoptera: Tortricidae)

Characteristics: Caterpillars large, plump, yellow orange, with a reddish-brown head. Adult moths large, slender, silver gray.

Habitat and range: Dunes in Oregon.

Comments: The caterpillars are deeply embedded among the flowers.

PLUME MOTH

(*Oidaematophorus* sp.: Lepidoptera: Pterophoridae)

Characteristics: Caterpillar pale cream, with a tan head and three red lines extending the length of the body. Pupa elongated, tan, slender, with legs exposed. Adult large, spindly, with long legs and extended narrow brown wings expanded at the tips.

Habitat and range: Dune systems from Washington to California.

Comments: The red stripes on the caterpillars are characteristic of many species and races of plume moths that feed on members of the Asteraceae family. The pupae differ from those of most moths in having exposed legs and a flexible abdomen that can bend almost 90 degrees.

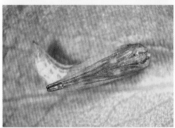

GREEN LEAF BEETLE

(*Trirhabda flavolimbata*: Coleoptera: Chrysomelidae)

Characteristics: Larvae black, elongated, with short legs. Adults have metallic-green wing covers with a narrow yellow margin, and a yellow pronotum bearing three dark spots.

Habitat and range: Dunes from Washington to California.

Comments: This species feeds on a number of plants in the Asteraceae family. The pupae occur in soil.

LEAF-MINING BEETLE
(*Monoxia* sp.: Coleoptera: Chrysomelidae)
Characteristics: Larva grayish black, with minute protrusions on the back. Adult small, slender, brownish, with darker markings on the wing covers.
Habitat and range: Dunes in Oregon and California.
Comments: The young larvae enter and mine the leaves but later keep just their heads under the leaf surface.

RED APHID
(*Uroleucon* sp.: Hemiptera: Aphididae)
Characteristics: Small, slender red aphids with black cornicles and black areas on the leg segments. Both parthenogenetic females and sexual adults occur on the same plant.
Habitat and range: Dunes in Oregon and California.
Comments: Other members of this aphid genus feed on goldenrod in eastern North America.

DUNE ORCHIDS

The dunes are not the most favorable place to look for orchids, but some hardy species are able to survive the wind and salt spray. It is always a surprise to encounter the delicate white flowers of bog rein orchid or hooded ladies tresses, especially when there was no sign of them several days previously. The elegant rein orchid survives on coastal bluffs overlooking the sea, but other orchids, like the stream orchid, prefer more typical habitats in the back dunes, together with other moisture-loving plants. Along the edges of dune woods is still another habitat, where the strikingly beautiful fairy slipper and camouflaged rattlesnake plantain reside.

Aside from some scale insects that pester commercially grown orchids, very few insect herbivores have been reported on wild North American orchids. Most insect associations with orchids relate to pollination, and orchids often take an active part in the process. Orchids produce pollen in small sacs called pollinia that are equipped with sticky appendages. When an insect enters the flower to obtain nectar, the pollinia are cemented to some part of its body (usually the head or back). When that insect visits another orchid, the pollinia are removed. In the case of the bog rein orchid, that insect is often a mosquito that probes the flowers for nectar and comes away with one or two pollinia attached to its head. These little pollinia are filled with individual pollen grains.

The structure of orchid flowers (especially the length and shape of the spur petal) as well as their fragrance often indicates the type of pollinator. Orchids that emit aromas during the night are pollinated by moths, while those releasing scents during the day will attract bees and flies. Moths appear to be the main pollinators of elegant rein orchids, while honeybees, bumblebees, and solitary bees carry pollinia of hooded ladies tresses, fairy slipper, and rattlesnake plantain, and flower flies pollinate stream orchids.

DUNE ORCHID COMMUNITY	
Orchids	Pollinators/Herbivores
Bog rein orchid	Mosquitoes
Elegant rein orchid	Moths
Rattlesnake plantain	Bees
Fairy slipper	Bumblebees
Stream orchid	Flower flies
Hooded ladies tresses	Seed beetles

BOG REIN ORCHID

(*Platanthera leucostachys*: Orchidaceae)

Characteristics: Stems erect, with appressed leaves, each stem bearing fragrant, spurred white flowers in straight rows (spikes).

Habitat and range: Dune areas and bogs from Washington to California and elsewhere.

Comments: Small mosquitoes of the genus *Aedes* (Diptera: Culicidae) serve as pollinators and transport pollen sacs (pollinia, lower left) filled with pollen grains they received while probing the flowers for nectar.

ELEGANT REIN ORCHID

(*Piperia elegans*: Orchidaceae)

Characteristics: Greenish-white flowers arranged in dense, straight or pyramidal clusters (spikes) arising from a single thick stem bearing a few short leaves.

Habitat and range: Dune areas, including sea bluffs and exposed meadows, from British Columbia to California.

Comments: The stems are especially short on exposed sandy bluffs in response to the constant winds. Pollinators include various moths.

RATTLESNAKE PLANTAIN

(*Goodyera oblongifolia*: Orchidaceae)

Characteristics: Leaves dark green with white streaks. Flowers pale yellow to greenish white, with an inflated lip.

Habitat and range: Borders of dune forests and mossy areas from Washington to California and elsewhere.

Comments: Pollinators include various bees.

FAIRY SLIPPER

(*Calypso bulbosa*: Orchidaceae)

Characteristics: Stem leafless, except for a single broad leaf at the base, bearing a solitary pinkish to red flower at the tip.

Habitat and range: Shady, moist habitats in the back dunes along edges of dune forests from Washington to California and elsewhere.

Comments: Fairy slipper can also be found in moist coniferous forests. Pollinators include bumblebees.

STREAM ORCHID

(*Epipactis gigantea*: Orchidaceae)

Characteristics: Stem leafy, with several yellowish-pink to reddish-purple flowers borne in upper leaf axils.

Habitat and range: Near dune seeps and ponds from Washington to California and elsewhere.

Comments: The petals often bear longitudinal red veins, and the thick flower stalks are usually curved. Pollinators include flower flies (Diptera: Syrphidae).

HOODED LADIES TRESSES

(*Spiranthes romanzoffiana*: Orchidaceae)

Characteristics: Perennial with one to three single stems; leaves linear to oblong at the base, reduced to narrow, sheathing bracts toward the top of the stem. Flowers white or greenish white, without spurs, borne in three to four spiraled rows. Fruits are capsules filled with many minute winged seeds.

Habitat and range: Dunes from Washington to California and elsewhere.

Comments: A beetle larva (Coleoptera: Melyridae, lower right) feeds on the seeds (lower left) of hooded ladies tresses. Pollinators include various types of bees.

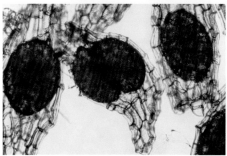 

DUNE PLANT COMMUNITIES: DUNE ORCHIDS

CREEPING BUTTERCUP

Dune depressions are frequently filled with water after the winter rains. When the water level falls to a few inches, small creeping buttercup plants quickly emerge and paint the landscape with splashes of bright yellow that stand out against the muddy bottom. Creeping buttercup must be one of the smallest, if not *the* smallest, of all the buttercups, and one of the few that has a creeping habit. The leaves are all linear, and the yellow flowers are so delicate that even a slight breeze can topple the ribbed petals and stamens. The plants send out horizontal stems in every direction, and these spread rapidly over the damp substrate. The plants attract aphids, which take up residence on the stems. The parthenogenetic females begin producing a continuous supply of minute nymphs, expelling them one after the other from the tip of their abdomen. Later, winged adults appear that will fly off and establish new colonies on neighboring plants. However, it doesn't take long for their presence to be noted by flower flies, whose maggots relish aphids. While many fall victim to the maggots, the aphids reproduce throughout the summer and the populations remain fairly stable.

CREEPING BUTTERCUP COMMUNITY	
Herbivores	Carnivores
Creeping buttercup aphid	Flower fly maggot

CREEPING BUTTERCUP
(*Ranunculus flammula*: Ranunculaceae)
Characteristics: Small perennial with trailing stems, narrow alternate leaves, and yellow flowers borne singly at the tips of erect stalks that emerge along the stems.
Habitat and range: Wet dune areas from Alaska to California and elsewhere.
Comments: This delicate species is considered poisonous and can cause dermatitis as well as digestive problems. Another buttercup that occurs on the dunes is the California buttercup (*Ranunculus californicus*), which has lobed leaves.

CREEPING BUTTERCUP APHID

(*Aphis* sp.: Hemiptera: Aphididae)

Characteristics: Small wingless parthenogenetic females are greenish, with red eyes and long brown legs, antennae, and cornicles. Winged forms are slightly larger and have a dark greenish head and thorax, clear membranous wings, and a tan abdomen with long cornicles.

Habitat and range: Dunes from Washington to California.

Comments: Flower fly maggots prey on the aphids.

PURPLE CUDWEED

Stroking the leaves of purple cudweed is like petting a bunny. The long leaves are covered with woolly white hairs that have a texture similar to that of animal hairs. The small flowers that appear from April to July are purple for only a short period and then become brownish. Purple cudweed has had several scientific names and is one of a growing number of plants for which the common name is more permanent than the scientific name. Aside from growing in dunes, purple cudweed also occurs on sandy bluffs and in fields. Both the aphid and caterpillar associated with cudweed feed deep within the purplish flowers. You will never notice them unless you pry apart the flower clusters.

PURPLE CUDWEED COMMUNITY
Herbivores
Flower caterpillar
Aphid

PURPLE CUDWEED
(*Gamochaeta ustulata* = *Gnaphalium purpureum*: Asteraceae)
Characteristics: Low-growing, hairy, annual to perennial herb with mostly spoon-shaped leaves that narrow toward the top. Flowers borne in dense terminal clusters, initially purple but soon turning brown.
Habitat and range: Dunes from British Columbia to California and elsewhere.
Comments: Cudweed often grows in clusters of three or more and is found in many different habitats besides the dunes.

FLOWER CATERPILLAR
(Lepidoptera: Noctuidae)

Characteristics: Small, lightly mottled tan caterpillar with sides bearing widely separated black dots.

Habitat and range: Dunes in Oregon.

Comments: The caterpillars live deep within the flower heads.

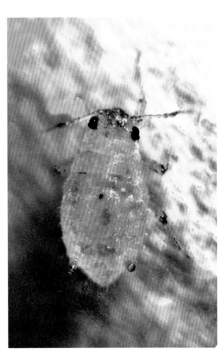

APHID
(*Aphis* sp.: Hemiptera: Aphididae)

Characteristics: Small, light green aphid with brownish eyes and short, straight cornicles.

Habitat and range: Dunes in Oregon and California.

Comments: These tiny aphids are usually hidden from view in the woolly hairs at the base of the flowers. Populations can become quite large.

DUNE PLANT COMMUNITIES: PURPLE CUDWEED

DUNE RUSH

Dune rush prefers damp sandy areas, especially in hollows in the foredunes, but also in the back dunes. Sometimes large colonies grow right at the high tide line. In some places, patches of dune rush have swollen reddish flower heads, quite different from the normal small brown ones. Inside these modified flower heads are populations of small jumping plant lice, or psyllids, crowded between the florets. These plant lice transform the dune rush flowers into galls that supply the insects with a continuous food supply and a secure home.

A secretive caterpillar feeding on dune rush escapes notice by living in a cigar-shaped case made out of chewed-up rush leaves glued together with saliva. With only its head exposed, the caterpillar feeds on the developing flower heads and is noticed only when its case starts shaking as it moves.

During late summer, another plant mysteriously springs up amid patches of dune rush. The colored flowers of the johnny-nip plant are quite beautiful and mask its lifestyle as a root parasite. It is easy to spot the red rust fungus on the leaves of dune rush. This is a fungus whose spores must infect a completely different plant to complete its life cycle. In this case, spores are carried by the wind to a plant in the Asteraceae family. Spores produced on this composite can then infect dune rush to complete the cycle.

DUNE RUSH COMMUNITY	
Herbivores	Parasites
Dune rush psyllid	Johnny-nip
Case moth	Red rust fungus

DUNE RUSH
(*Juncus effusus*: Juncaceae)
Characteristics: Grass-like perennial with cylindrical stems; cylindrical to flat, long, slender leaves; and long rhizomes. Flowers small and brownish, forming in dense clusters at the tips of the stems.
Habitat and range: Wet dune areas and coastal tide flats from Alaska to Baja California.
Comments: Dune rush prefers damp areas along the coast but can also survive near the tide line.

DUNE RUSH PSYLLID

(*Livia caricis*: Hemiptera: Psyllidae)

Characteristics: Nymphs small, pale yellow, with dark eyes and antennae. Adults small and greenish yellow, with gray eyes, short antennae and legs, and thick elliptical wings.

Habitat and range: Dunes from Washington to California and elsewhere.

Comments: This psyllid develops in flower buds, which it transforms into galls (upper left).

CASE MOTH

(*Coleophora* sp.: Lepidoptera: Coleophoridae)

Characteristics: The small brownish caterpillars construct cases made from bits of rush glued together with their saliva.

Habitat and range: Dunes in Oregon.

Comments: The caterpillars remain in their cases when feeding on dune rush flowers.

JOHNNY-NIP

(*Castilleja ambigua*: Scrophulariaceae)

Characteristics: Annual herb growing among patches of dune rush. The flower heads have large bracts interspersed with small yellow flowers. The small stem leaves are reddish green.

Habitat and range: Dunes from British Columbia to California.

Comments: Johnny-nip is considered a semiparasite on the roots of dune rush.

RED RUST FUNGUS

(*Uromyces* sp.: Uredinales: Pucciniaceae)

Characteristics: Small, elongated, reddish infected areas on the leaves of dune rush. Each area contains masses of thick-walled fungal spores with miniature spines on their surfaces.

Habitat and range: Dunes from Washington to California.

Comments: This rust fungus alternates between two hosts, dune rush and members of the aster or sunflower family.

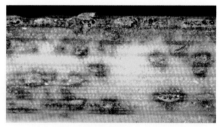

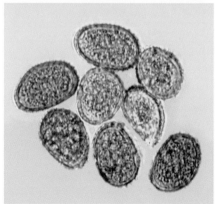

YELLOW BUSH LUPINE

You can't miss the yellow-flowered spikes of yellow bush lupine, especially in its prime habitat in northern California. It is a favorite of deer, gophers, and rabbits, and even some birds partake of the seeds. Its foliage is eaten by salt marsh, tussock, and silver-tipped woolly caterpillars. Yellow bush lupine is native to southern California, but it is considered an invasive plant on dunes in Mendocino and Humboldt Counties and was one of the plants removed in a northern California eradication program that attempted to reestablish the native dune flora.

Although originally planted along the coast as a dune stabilizer, it has formed dense, impenetrable groves that reach up to six feet tall. A gall gnat has the ability to turn the leaflets of yellow bush lupine into podlike structures. But instead of being filled with seeds, these "pods" contain a slimy secretion with masses of small, squirming yellow maggots. Seed weevils, stem maggots, and leaf and pod moths also take their toll.

In the stems and roots of yellow bush lupine lives the secretive ghost moth caterpillar. One would imagine that living inside woody stems would offer a secure dwelling that kept enemies out. However, parasitic wasps and small parasitic nematodes have been able to penetrate this barrier. The caterpillars maintain their normal coloration when parasitized by wasp larvae, but they turn red with nematode infections.

YELLOW BUSH LUPINE COMMUNITY	
Herbivores	Parasites
Leaf gall gnat	Wasps
Silver-tipped woolly caterpillar	Nematodes
Ghost moth caterpillar	
Seed weevil	
Stem maggot	
Leaf and pod moth	
Deer, rabbits, gophers	

YELLOW BUSH LUPINE

(*Lupinus arboreus*: Fabaceae)

Characteristics: Dense, shrubby bush with glabrous dark green leaves divided into five to twelve leaflets. Petals large, yellow. Fruit a hairy pod.

Habitat and range: Dunes in Oregon and California.

Comments: This species hybridizes with other dune lupines and sometimes has lilac-tinted petals. The related shrubby coastal species *Lupinus chamissonis* has dense, silver-haired leaflets and violet to blue flowers. The latter species is restricted to California dunes and is attacked by tortricid moths and stem flies.

LEAF GALL GNAT

(*Dasineura lupinorum*: Diptera: Cecidomyiidae)

Characteristics: Small, cream to yellow larvae within swollen leaflet galls. Adult gnats small, fragile, with transparent wings.

Habitat and range: Dunes in California.

Comments: The galls cause the leaflets to swell up and the edges to curve inward and meet tightly along the middle, imitating pods. The conditions inside are quite moist, and the larvae, which often occur in groups of ten or more, can tolerate a semiliquid habitat.

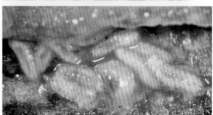

SILVER-TIPPED WOOLLY CATERPILLAR

(*Platyprepia virginalis*: Lepidoptera: Arctiidae)

Characteristics: Very large black caterpillar with orange hairs at the anterior and posterior ends, and black hairs mixed with long white hairs in the middle of the body.
Habitat and range: Occurs in dunes and other habitats from Canada to California.
Comments: The caterpillars, which feed on a wide range of plants, are usually solitary and are quite conspicuous.

GHOST MOTH CATERPILLAR

(*Hepialus californicus*: Lepidoptera: Hepialidae)

Characteristics: Large, pale tan caterpillar with scattered dark brown spots covering the body and pronotum.
Habitat and range: Dunes in California.
Comments: The caterpillars, which occur in the roots and lower stems, are parasitized by nematodes (*Heterorhabditis* sp.) and wasps. After killing the caterpillar, the wasp larva forms a white cocoon adjacent to the remains of its victim.

SEED WEEVIL

(*Apion proclive*: Coleoptera: Brentidae)

Characteristics: Small, legless white larva with a brown head and curved body. Adult small, uniformly gray, with a long, slender beak and striated elytra.
Habitat and range: Dunes in California.
Comments: The developing larvae destroy the seeds within the pods.

STEM MAGGOT

(*Agromyza* sp.: Diptera: Agromyzidae)
Characteristics: Small, stocky, elongated white maggots with black mouth hooks. The puparia are reddish brown, with a darkened anterior end.
Habitat and range: Dunes in California.
Comments: The maggots and puparia occur in the stems.

LEAF AND POD MOTH

(*Epinotia infuscana*: Lepidoptera: Tortricidae)
Characteristics: Caterpillar whitish, with a dark pronotum and head. Adult moth large, light brown, with subdued reddish-tan areas on the wings.
Habitat and range: Dunes in California.
Comments: The caterpillars develop in curled leaves as well as in seedpods.

BRACKEN FERN

Ferns reproduce by spores, and the arrangement of the spores on the leaves (called pinnae in ferns) aids in identification. Groups of spores are called sori, and these are usually arranged in little brown clusters on the undersides of the leaves.

One would think that herbivores that feed on ferns would be rare, because ferns contain distasteful chemical compounds in order to repel herbivores. For instance, bracken fern, which is quite common in the dunes, stores cyanide in its leaves, which explains why ranchers want to keep it out of their pastures. But these chemicals don't stop insects from feeding on bracken. A number of moth caterpillars, usually those that are known to browse on other plants, also dine on bracken leaves. But there are insects that appear to be specific to bracken fern.

One of the most fascinating is the bracken leaf gall gnat. On one large, sandy, exposed knoll overlooking the ocean grows a patch of bracken that rarely exceeds a yard in height. Some of the leaves appear to have burnt tips. Peeling back the coal-black "burnt" portion of the leaf, I exposed tiny orange fly larvae and pupae. Apparently, this leaf gall gnat had never been officially reported from North America before, but there is one with similar habits in Europe. When and how it arrived here is a mystery.

Another gall gnat makes mines between the veins of the leaves. Each mine is also inhabited by a white fungus, whose relationship with the gall gnat remains unknown. Spiny galls on the tips of the leaves are made by leaf-folding moth caterpillars, which stimulate the growing tissues of the leaves to develop abnormally. Even in these domiciles, the caterpillars are targeted by parasitic wasps.

BRACKEN FERN COMMUNITY	
Herbivores	Parasites
Leaf gall gnat	White fungus
Leaf curl fly	Wasps
Short-nosed weevil	
Leaf mine gall gnat	
Green-lined caterpillar	
Two-lined leaf roller	
Terminal leaf gall moth	
Bracken aphid	
Rusty tussock moth caterpillar	
Woolly bear caterpillar	
White-spotted caterpillar	
White-banded inchworm	

BRACKEN FERN

(*Pteridium aquilinum*: Dennstaedtiacae)
Characteristics: Large deciduous perennial with erect triangular leaves (fronds)
that are divided two to three times. Leaflets
(pinnae) opposite, hairy beneath, with
margins inrolled. Spores borne in rows on
underside of leaf margins.
Habitat and range: Cosmopolitan, including dunes from Washington to California.
Comments: Bracken occurs worldwide
and is used by a number of insect
herbivores.

LEAF GALL GNAT

(*Dasineura* sp.: Diptera: Cecidomyiidae)
Characteristics: Maggot minute, white,
with black mouth hooks; prepupa and pupa
elliptical, yellowish orange.
Habitat and range: Dunes in Oregon.
Comments: The larvae develop as
leaf miners along the edge of the fern
leaflet. The prepupae and pupae somehow
stimulate the edges of the fern leaflet to
harden and curve around them. Adults
were not obtained. This is the first record
of this association in North America. An
Old World species, *Dasineura filicina*, causes
similar galls on bracken fern in Europe.

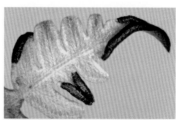

LEAF CURL FLY

(*Chirosia idahensis*: Diptera: Anthomyiidae)

Characteristics: Adult flies small, grayish, with large dark eyes and clear wings. Larvae white, with black mouth hooks. Pupae formed in the soil.

Habitat and range: Western North America.

Comments: The feeding action of the larvae causes the tips of the developing leaflets to curve inward and form a dense green gall.

SHORT-NOSED WEEVIL

(*Nemocestes tuberculatus*: Coleoptera: Curculionidae)

Characteristics: A small, stout brown weevil with a short, blunt beak.

Habitat and range: Dunes in Oregon.

Comments: The larvae feed on various roots and the adults feed on bracken foliage.

LEAF MINE GALL GNAT

(*Mycodiplosis* sp.: Diptera: Cecidomyiidae)

Characteristics: Larvae minute, oval, yellowish.

Habitat and range: Dunes in Oregon.

Comments: The larvae occur between the veins and feed on bracken tissue that is infected with a white fungus, thus giving the galls a white appearance. Details of this association are unclear.

GREEN-LINED CATERPILLAR

(*Phlogophora* sp.: Lepidoptera: Noctuidae)

Characteristics: Very large, grayish-green caterpillar with a tan head and dark, V-shaped lines on its back.

Habitat and range: Throughout North America.

Comments: The caterpillars are generalist feeders on broad-leaved plants as well as ferns.

TWO-LINED LEAF ROLLER

(Lepidoptera: Tortricidae)

Characteristics: A large, light green caterpillar with a tan head and two broad, cream-colored bands running the length of the body.

Habitat and range: Dunes in Oregon.

Comments: The caterpillars feed within shelters they make by folding over the edges of leaves with webbing. The brown pupae are formed within the shelters.

TERMINAL LEAF GALL MOTH

(*Acleris* sp.: Lepidoptera: Tortricidae)

Characteristics: Caterpillar small, reddish, with a dark brown head and thorax. Pupa dark brown. Adult large, reddish brown, with a V-shaped pattern over the closed forewings.

Habitat and range: Dunes in Oregon.

Comments: The feeding action of the larvae causes the tips of the fronds to curl inward and form a loose gall.

BRACKEN APHID

(*Macrosiphum* sp.: Hemiptera: Aphididae)

Characteristics: Hermaphroditic females small, dark green. Nymphs slender, pale green to yellow.

Habitat and range: Dunes in Oregon, but the genus is widespread.

Comments: Large populations can build up on bracken.

RUSTY TUSSOCK MOTH CATERPILLAR

(*Orgyria antiqua*: Lepidoptera: Arctiidae)

Characteristics: Caterpillar large, dark brown, covered with tufts of yellow hairs arising from pinkish body tubercles. Four large tufts of white hairs are positioned behind the head.

Habitat and range: Dunes in Oregon, but the species is widespread.

Comments: This species has a wide range of hosts, and bracken is probably only occasionally used as a food plant.

WOOLLY BEAR CATERPILLAR

(*Spilosoma virginica*: Lepidoptera: Arctiidae)

Characteristics: Caterpillar large, gray, each segment covered with tufts of long, reddish-tan hairs.

Habitat and range: Dunes in Oregon, but the species is widespread.

Comments: This species has a wide host range, and bracken is probably only occasionally used as a food plant.

WHITE-SPOTTED CATERPILLAR

(*Phlogophora* sp.: Lepidoptera: Noctuidae)

Characteristics: Very large, robust, completely green caterpillar with a pair of white spots near the posterior end.

Habitat and range: Dunes in Oregon.

Comments: The presence of white spots is curious when the rest of the body is camouflaged in green.

WHITE-BANDED INCHWORM

(Lepidoptera: Geometridae)

Characteristics: Large, dark brown caterpillar with a broad, wavy white band running along both sides of the body.

Habitat and range: Dunes in Oregon.

Comments: The striking color pattern of this caterpillar boldly contrasts against the green fern leaves.

SHORE PINE

Shore pine is the most common conifer on sand dunes from Washington to northern California, sometimes growing not far from the high tide level. It is an example of how a plant can modify its growth habits depending on the surroundings. On flat, exposed sand dunes, mature trees with cones can be less than three feet high. But in the mountains, the same species, which is called lodgepole pine, can tower over 150 feet high. Intermediate forms grow at various elevations and habitats in between the coast and the mountains.

One noticeable herbivore on shore pine is the silver-spotted tiger moth. The large, black-banded caterpillars are quite social and spin common webbing for protection as they feed on the needles. They spend only their short developmental period together and then disperse to construct hairy cocoons for pupation. When so many caterpillars are together on one pine branch, it is easy for parasitic wasps and tachinid flies to detect them. But despite these foes, as well as lethal viruses that can devastate entire populations, the caterpillars return each spring.

Tiger moth caterpillars are not the only social insects devouring the pine needles. Gregarious larvae of green- and white-striped pine sawflies share that habitat. Caterpillars of the pine elfin butterfly and pine-tip moth also feed on the needles, while caterpillars of the minute pine needle sheath miner start life inside individual pine needles, eventually coming out to gnaw away on the needles. Red turpentine beetles and western subterranean termites devour the wood, while small caterpillars feed on the cones. Spittlebugs and aphids live on the needles and suck the plant's sap, and where there are aphids there are always predaceous flower fly larvae.

A number of mushrooms depend on shore pine, and many of these have symbiotic mycorrhizal associations with the trees. In some cases, the fungus constructs a sheath around the rootlets of the pine to obtain nutrients and moisture. In return, the fungus supplies the pine with minerals. But these relationships are complicated, since other fungi, such as the wind-cap mushroom, can parasitize the mycorrhizae. Such associations have been going on underground for eons, with the only aboveground evidence being mushrooms that emerge in the vicinity of shore pines.

Some mushrooms that have mycorrhizal relationships, such as the king bolete, grow erect and release their spores from gills, while others, like the potato mushroom, are subterrestrial, with only the tops of their saclike fruiting bodies exposed to allow the spores to escape. Various invertebrates, such as scavenger and sap beetles, fungus gnats, and banana slugs, suddenly appear to feed on the fruiting bodies of these mushrooms.

Chickarees often ascend the trees and perch on the branches within reach of pinecones, which they easily tear apart and eat. They hold the ends of the cone with their claws and continuously turn it around, just like a human eating an ear of corn.

SHORE PINE COMMUNITY	
Herbivores	Parasites/Predators/Symbionts
Silver-spotted tiger moth	Tachinid fly
Shore pine sawfly	Parasitic wasp
Pine elfin	Virus
Pine-tip moth	Flower fly
Pine needle sheath miner	King bolete
Red turpentine beetle	Scavenger beetle
Dwarf bark beetle	Wine-cap mushroom
Spotted pinecone moth	Banana slug
Blotched pinecone caterpillar	Potato mushroom
Western pine spittlebug	Sap beetle
Conifer aphid	Mites
Pine woolly aphid	Nematodes
Chickaree	Fungus gnats
	Gall gnat larva

SHORE PINE
(*Pinus contorta*: Pinaceae)
Characteristics: Evergreen pine tree growing alone or in dense clumps. Leaves needlelike, with two leaves to a bundle. Male cones reddish, clustered at the base of new growth. Female cones developing beneath, usually single and often remaining on the tree for several years.
Habitat and range: Various dune habitats from Alaska to northern California.
Comments: This is the most common dune conifer north of Humboldt Bay, California. Other conifers in coastal habitats, such as sitka spruce (*Picea sitchensis*), Douglas-fir (*Pseudotsuga menziesii*), western hemlock (*Tsuga heterophylla*), and coastal redwood (*Sequoia sempervirens*), occur mostly in dune forests or on ridges overlooking the ocean. Monterey pine (*Pinus radiata*) and Monterey cypress (*Cupressus macrocarpa*) sometimes grow along the coast but are confined to the Monterey Peninsula in California.

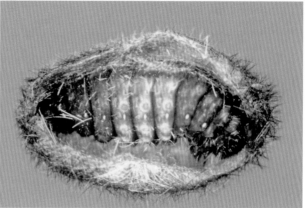

SILVER-SPOTTED TIGER MOTH

(*Lophocampa argentata*: Lepidoptera: Arctiidae)

Characteristics: Mature caterpillars large, with variable coloration, mostly with alternating black and yellow areas separated by tufts of yellow and reddish-brown hairs. Cocoon made with silk and body hairs. Adults very large, colored shades of brown, with bold white spots on the forewings.

Habitat and range: British Columbia to California.

Comments: Eggs hatch in the fall, and the young caterpillars, which congregate in silken webs, overwinter and finish feeding in May and June. The caterpillars are parasitized by tachinid flies (*Uramya halisidotae*: Diptera: Tachinidae) and attacked by nuclear polyhedrosis viruses.

SHORE PINE SAWFLY

(*Neodiprion annulus contortae*: Hymenoptera: Diprionidae)

Characteristics: Mature larvae large, with a black head and olive-green body with lighter longitudinal stripes. Cocoons dark brown. Adults large, black or dark brown, with transparent wings and tan legs. Males have feathery antennae.

Habitat and range: From Canada to Oregon along the coast.

Comments: The larvae occur in colonies and can defoliate entire branches. They are attacked by parasitic wasps and flies.

PINE ELFIN

(*Callophrys eryphon*: Lepidoptera: Lycaenidae)

Characteristics: Adults large and brown, with some white and tan cross lines on the forewings. Caterpillars green, sluglike, with short fuzzy hairs and yellow stripes.

Habitat and range: Throughout northwestern North America.

Comments: This is one of the few butterflies that develop on pines. The caterpillars devour the pine needles and often occur in groups.

PINE-TIP MOTH

(*Choristoneura* sp.: Lepidoptera: Tortricidae)

Characteristics: Adults are large and mottled gray brown, with two broken darker bands across the forewings.

Habitat and range: Western North America.

Comments: The caterpillars live in the tips of branches. A similar moth occurs in stem cankers on the branches of shore pine.

PINE NEEDLE SHEATH MINER
(*Zelleria haimbachi*: Lepidoptera: Yponomeutidae)

Characteristics: First-stage caterpillar long and narrow. Pupa small, narrow, brown. Adult small, narrow, uniformly light yellowish brown, with a dark band along the edge of each wing.

Habitat and range: Washington to California and elsewhere in North America.

Comments: Early-stage caterpillars feed inside pine needles. Later-stage caterpillars feed at the base of needle clusters, which are eventually severed. The pupae are formed within cavities carved out of the bases of several pine needles. The slender adults with wings held tightly against their bodies are well camouflaged and mimic dried pine needles.

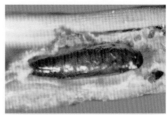

RED TURPENTINE BEETLE
(*Dendroctonus valens*: Coleoptera: Scolytidae)

Characteristics: Larvae white, legless, C-shaped, with a tan head. Adults small, pale to dark red, with pale hairs on the head and back.

Habitat and range: Throughout North America.

Comments: Red turpentine beetles attack healthy as well as dead or dying pines. They lay their eggs in galleries under the bark and the larvae feed on the inner bark. Mites and nematodes live in the larval galleries.

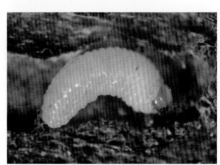

DWARF BARK BEETLE

(*Dolurgus pumilus*: Coleoptera: Scolytidae)

Characteristics: A very small, cylindrical brown beetle (under 2 mm long) with a small head partly covered by the thorax, small clubbed antennae, and small emarginate eyes.

Habitat and range: Throughout the Pacific Northwest from Alaska to northern California.

Comments: This beetle attacks dying trees but enters the bark through holes made by larger bark beetles such as the red turpentine beetle, which is three to four times the size of the dwarf bark beetle.

SPOTTED PINECONE MOTH

(*Dioryctria* sp.: Lepidoptera: Pyralidae)

Characteristics: Caterpillar small, light brown, with rows of small dark brown spots on its body. Pupa reddish brown, forms inside cone. Adult moth small, grayish brown, with light and dark areas, including a dark brown crescent on the closed wings not far behind the head.

Habitat and range: Throughout western North America.

Comments: A number of moth caterpillars develop in shore pine cones. The small, extremely well-camouflaged blotched pinecone caterpillar (*Eucosma* sp.: Lepidoptera: Tortricidae) also feeds on the female cones (bottom left).

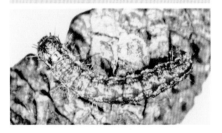

WESTERN PINE SPITTLEBUG

(*Aphrophora permutata*: Hemiptera: Cercopidae)

Characteristics: Mature nymphs are small and reddish brown, with a white head and short black antennae. Adults are mottled brown, with clusters of spines on their legs.

Habitat and range: British Columbia to California and other western states.

Comments: This spittlebug feeds on other pines as well as shore pine. The nymphs surround themselves with spittle-like froth on the pine twigs.

CONIFER APHID

(*Cinara* spp.: Hemiptera: Aphididae)

Characteristics: Small, reddish-brown aphids with long legs and antennae and a smooth body.

Habitat and range: The genus is global, with high diversity in western North America.

Comments: Conifer aphids can be solitary or gregarious. Dune ants (*Formica* sp.: Hymenoptera: Formicidae) attend the aphids to obtain honeydew. Yellowish-green flower fly larvae (*Eupeodes* sp.: Diptera: Syrphidae) attack the aphids. Adult flower flies have a large, dark body crossed with yellow bars, and large eyes.

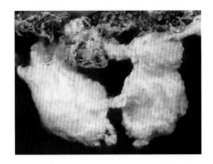

PINE WOOLLY APHID

(*Adelges* sp.: Hemiptera: Aphididae)

Characteristics: Small aphids covered with cottony white tufts of wax.

Habitat and range: Back dunes in Oregon.

Comments: These aphids live within cottony white tufts attached to pine needles and only lay eggs. Gall gnat larvae (*Diadiplosis* sp.: Diptera: Cecidomyiidae) parasitize pine woolly aphids.

KING BOLETE

(*Boletus edulis*: Boletaceae)

Characteristics: Mushroom with a convex, reddish-brown cap, a brownish-yellow undersurface covered with pores, and a firm, thick white stalk that can become reddish brown.

Habitat and range: Cosmopolitan.

Comments: Shiny black scavenger beetles (*Necrophilus hydrophiloides*: Coleoptera: Agyrtidae) feed on the stalks of king bolete.

WINE-CAP MUSHROOM

(*Chroogomphus vinicolor*: Gomphidiaceae)

Characteristics: Cap conical, dull orange brownish, smooth. Gills broad, whitish to tan. Stalk slender, brownish. Veil dry, not persisting.

Habitat and range: Widespread in North America.

Comments: This mushroom, which is a parasite of the mycorrhizae of the king bolete, is sought out by Pacific banana slugs (*Ariolimax columbianus*: Arionidae).

POTATO MUSHROOM

(*Rhizopogon* sp.: Rhizopogonaceae)

Characteristics: A stalkless, saclike underground mushroom that exposes its top portion for spore release. Surface covered with fine black fungal strands (rhizomorphs). Spore mass spongelike, yellowish.

Habitat and range: Widespread under conifers.

Comments: Yellow sap beetle larvae (*Epuraea* sp.: Coleoptera: Nitidulidae) develop in the spore mass. Black adult sap beetles are usually somewhere nearby. Squirrels and fungus gnats also feed on potato mushrooms.

CHICKAREE

(*Tamiasciurus douglasi*: Sciuridae)

Characteristics: A dune squirrel that is dark reddish above, with a yellowish-red belly. Distinct black line along each side (indistinct in winter).

Habitat and range: Washington to California in dunes and coniferous forests.

Comments: The diet consists mainly of conifer cones, including those of shore pine, which are held like a cob of corn. They also eat fruits, mushrooms, acorns, and even bird eggs.

WESTERN BLUE VIOLET

How pleasing it is when the western blue violets began to bloom in grassy clearings within the dunes or along forest edges. At first they appear stemless, with leaves and flower stalks arising separately from the ground, but eventually the stems appear, if the plants are not eaten first. A number of moth caterpillars, such as the bristly ornate tiger moth caterpillar, relish blue violets. You don't want to touch the stiff hairs covering this caterpillar. It feels like it can throw its hairs into your skin, similar to the story of how porcupines can release their quills. Yet out of the smooth tan pupa that forms at the base of the violet plant emerges a moth with such striking wing markings that you might assume it was part of a canvas by one of the impressionists.

Unfortunately, populations of the western blue violet are disappearing, and that is also disastrous for the caterpillars of butterflies that depend on this plant. One such example is the endangered Oregon silverspot, one of several fritillaries that exist on this plant.

WESTERN BLUE VIOLET COMMUNITY
Herbivores
Ornate tiger moth
Cutworm
Oregon silverspot butterfly

WESTERN BLUE VIOLET
(*Viola adunca*: Violaceae)
Characteristics: Short perennial growing close to the ground in exposed areas. Leaves oval to heart shaped, with scalloped margins. Flowers violet to purple; petals, especially the lower one, with longitudinal dark veins. Fruit a small, three-valved capsule.
Habitat and range: In back dunes and dune forests from Washington to California.
Comments: Early blue violet is the food plant for three federally endangered or threatened rare butterflies.

ORNATE TIGER MOTH

(*Grammia ornata*: Lepidoptera: Arctiidae)

Characteristics: Large mature caterpillars quite bristly, with a series of hair clumps along both sides of the back and on the sides. Lateral and dorsal hair clumps gray, ventral hairs orange. Pupae comparatively wide, reddish. Adults very large, with light brown to black forewings with crossing yellow bars and lines.

Habitat and range: In back dunes and forest clearings from Washington to California.

Comments: Wing patterns vary somewhat. The caterpillars feed on other plants besides violets.

CUTWORM

(*Lacinipolia olivacea*: Lepidoptera: Noctuidae)

Characteristics: Mature caterpillars are large and uniformly pale brown, but somewhat lighter beneath. The head is tan and the spiracles are black. Adults are large, stocky, with brown forewings bearing light markings.

Habitat and range: In back dunes and clear-cuts of dune forests from Washington to California.

Comments: While these caterpillars are generalists, they often denude the foliage of western blue violets.

OREGON SILVERSPOT BUTTERFLY

(*Speyeria zerene*: Lepidoptera: Nymphalidae)

Characteristics: Mature caterpillars large, gray to black, with rows of spiny cones arising from the body segments. Adults very large, with wings covered with a series of irregular white and brown spots over an orange-brown background.

Habitat and range: Meadows and clearings in dune forests in Oregon and California.

Comments: The adults feed on nectar from a number of flowers growing in the same habitat. Oregon silverspot is rare and considered a vulnerable species (likely to become endangered) by the International Union for Conservation of Nature.

SPRINGBANK CLOVER

This beautiful clover plant, also called marsh clover, ranges from British Columbia to Mexico along the coast on beaches, dunes, or the edges of salt marshes. One of the first herbivores I found on springbank clover was a sawfly larva along the central Oregon coast that was devouring the leaves. Even after examining many populations from Washington to northern California (Lake Earl), I never found this sawfly again. This shows how selective some insects can be regarding their habitat. In the life of every organism, there is a time to eat, a time to reproduce, a time to disperse, and a time to disappear. Species extinctions may take millions of years, but sooner or later, they will occur. A number of insects occurred at other sites I visited, showing that springbank clover is highly desirable. These included a number of caterpillars as well as leaf and seed weevils.

SPRINGBANK CLOVER COMMUNITY	
Herbivores	Carnivores/Parasites
Leaf weevil	Beach water beetle
Seed weevil	Dodder
Sawfly	
Inchworm	
Striped caterpillar	
Green flower caterpillar	
Flower butterfly	
White caterpillar moth	

SPRINGBANK CLOVER
(*Trifolium wormskjoldii*: Fabaceae)
Characteristics: A perennial clover with trifid leaves and large red, pink, or purple flowers.
Habitat and range: In wet and moist dune areas from Washington to northern California.
Comments: The plants spread by stolons and often occur in large groups. They grow in grassy meadows as well as in saturated soil close to the ocean.

LEAF WEEVIL
(*Hypera punctata*: Coleoptera: Curculionidae)
Characteristics: Larvae grayish green, legless; pupae white; adults brown, small, stout, and flightless, with a short, thick beak.
Habitat and range: Meadows and back dunes along the coast from Washington to California and elsewhere.
Comments: This species first appeared in eastern North America as an immigrant from Europe. It then worked its way west and now occurs throughout the continent, feeding on a number of clover species.

SEED WEEVIL
(*Miccotrogus picirostris*: Coleoptera: Curculionidae)
Characteristics: A small, slender black weevil covered with whitish scales. Beak black, slender, slightly curved, as long as the pronotum.
Habitat and range: Occurs along the coast from Washington to northern California and elsewhere.
Comments: This introduced European species feeds on a number of different clovers. The larvae develop in the seeds and can be quite destructive.

SAWFLY

(*Nematus atriceps*: Hymenoptera: Tenthredinidae)

Characteristics: Larva green, medium sized, with a brownish head; pupa completely green except for black eyes, with legs and antennae free, formed in an oval brown cocoon ; adult medium sized, with a black head and thorax, yellow legs, and yellow abdomen with transverse black bars.

Habitat and range: Found in wet habitats in Oregon.

Comments: The larvae prefer to feed on the leaves but form their cocoons on the flowers.

STRIPED CATERPILLAR

(Lepidoptera: Noctuidae)

Characteristics: Mature caterpillars very large, with a green head and a body bearing a series of wide, longitudinal brown lines, each of a different shade.

Habitat and range: Back dunes in California and Oregon.

Comments: The color, shades, and thickness of the stripes vary between individuals. They feed on the leaves and flowers. Adults were not obtained.

INCHWORM
(Lepidoptera: Geometridae)

Characteristics: Mature caterpillar large, brown, with a series of diamond-shaped reddish patches along the back and two pairs of posterior prolegs.

Habitat and range: Back dunes in Oregon and California.

Comments: They feed on both flowers and leaves. Adults were not obtained.

GREEN FLOWER CATERPILLAR
(Lepidoptera: Noctuidae)

Characteristics: Medium-sized, completely green caterpillar with a sparse covering of long, straight hairs over its body.

Habitat and range: Back dunes in Oregon.

Comments: These caterpillars feed within the flower heads, which makes them rather conspicuous when exposed. Adults were not obtained.

FLOWER BUTTERFLY
(*Plebejus saepiolus*: Lepidoptera: Lycaenidae)

Characteristics: Caterpillar small, stocky, cream colored, with a few faint longitudinal red stripes on the body. Adult with dark brown wing surfaces, and wing undersides cream colored with a series of dark spots.

Habitat and range: Sandy meadows near the sea in central Oregon and northern California.

Comments: The wing colors differ between the sexes, being blue in the males and dark brown to reddish in the females. The coloring on the undersurfaces of the wings is similar in both sexes. The caterpillars are quite inconspicuous and easily overlooked.

WHITE CATERPILLAR MOTH

(*Grapholita conversana*: Lepidoptera: Tortricidae)

Characteristics: Caterpillar medium sized, completely white except for the tan head capsule. Pupa formed in a thick white cocoon on the ground. Adult moth medium sized, black except for white markings on the wings and white leg spurs.

Habitat and range: Dunes from Washington to California and elsewhere.

Comments: The caterpillars feed deep within the clover flower heads.

BEACH WATER BEETLE

(*Hydrotrupes palpalis*: Coleoptera: Dytiscidae)

Characteristics: Small, broadly oval, shiny black beetle with short antennae and minute punctures on the back.

Habitat and range: Among the roots of springbank clover in Oregon and Washington.

Comments: These beetles commonly occur in habitats covered by a thin film of water, which explains their presence among the roots of springbank clover growing in such locations. Beach water beetles are predaceous and feed on various moisture-loving invertebrates, especially midge larvae.

DODDER

(*Cuscuta* sp.: Cuscutaceae)

Characteristics: The plants consist of twisty yellow stems bearing clusters of small white flowers at intervals. There are no recognizable leaves, only small protuberances for penetrating into the clover plant.

Habitat and range: Throughout the Pacific Northwest on various plants besides springbank clover.

Comments: Both clovers and lupines (see seaside lupine) are attacked by dodder, indicating that perhaps leguminous plants are favored hosts.

GLOSSARY OF TERMS

Abdomen—the third or terminal body portion of an insect.

Acanthocephalan—a spiny-headed parasitic worm that lives, as an adult, in vertebrates.

Achene—a dry, one-seeded fruit.

Alate—winged, as an insect.

Alternate leaves—borne at different levels on the stem.

Annual—a plant that grows from seed to maturity and death in one season.

Antennae—paired sensory organs or "feelers" attached to the head of an arthropod.

Anther—the pollen-bearing part of the stamen.

Apex (*pl.* **apices**)—the tip of a structure.

Apical—outermost tip.

Aposematic colors—bright colors that advertise that the bearer contains toxic compounds and is not edible.

Awn—a bristlelike appendage.

Back dune—dune region that extends from the perennial shrub region at the end of the middune to the first dwarf trees. These dwarf trees may then merge with established trees as part of a dune forest.

Bark beetle—a small beetle living and feeding within the bark or wood of plants.

Basal—located at the bottom, as on a stem.

Beach—land along the seashore, often between the high- and low-water marks, but can also include the foredune.

Beak—extended hardened mouthparts, as in birds and some insects.

Biennial—a plant that grows from seed to maturity and death in two seasons.

Bilabiate—two-lipped, as a petal.

Biological control—using insects and other living organisms to control unwanted plants and insect pests.

Biota—the plants and animals in an area.

Bloom—a white deposit on a surface.

Brood—the accumulated young of an insect, especially pertaining to bees.

Browsers—animals that sample different plants.

Calyx—the basal circle of floral elements.

Camouflage—protective coloring that allows an organism to blend into the background.

Campanulate—bell-shaped.

Capsule—a dry fruit that splits open at maturity.

Carapace—the hard shell of a crab or other arthropod.

Carnivore—an animal that feeds on other animals.

Carrion—decaying animal flesh.

Caterpillar—active juvenile stage between the egg and pupa of a moth or butterfly.

Catkin—a scaly-clustered row of flowers, as in willows.

Caudal—at the tail end.

Cauline—pertaining to the stem.

Cerci—a pair of appendages near the tip of an insect's abdomen.

Chrysalis—the pupal stage of a butterfly.

Ciliate—fringed with small hairs.

Circumglobal—occurring around the world.

Coast—land bordering the sea.

Coastal dunes—sand dunes along the sea.

Cocoon—a protective case, often hairy or silky, spun by an insect larva as a place for pupation.

Commensalism—an association between two organisms in which one benefits and the other is not harmed.

Composite—a plant of the sunflower family.

Conk—a hard fruiting body of a fungus, usually attached to a tree.

Cornicles—tubular structures emerging from the abdomen of aphids that emit defensive and alarm compounds.

Corolla—inner floral circle composed of petals.

Cosmopolitan—occurring everywhere.

Coxa—first segment of an insect's leg adjacent to its body.

Crustacean—many-legged land and marine invertebrate that breathes by gills and has a hard body covering and more than eight legs.

Cutworm—the immature stage of a moth, usually belonging to the family Noctuidae.

Deciduous—falling, as in autumn leaves.

Decumbent—stretched along the ground.

Definitive host—an animal in which a parasite matures and reproduces.

Deflation plain—lower area or depression that often retains moisture and is inhabited by a unique group of plants and animals.

Dehiscence—how a seedpod or anther opens.

Detritivore—an organism that feeds on dead and decaying material.

Diapause—a period of arrested development, often caused by excessive heat or cold.

Disease—a disturbance in the function or structure of an organ or tissue.

Disk florets—tubular, centrally positioned florets in the flower heads of members of the sunflower family.

Diurnal—active in the daytime.

Dorsal or **dorsum**—the back of an object.

Downy—covered with short, soft hairs.

Driftwood—a general term for all shapes and sizes of wooden objects that are washed up on the beach.

Dune—sandy area adjacent to the sea.

Dune forest—areas of sand behind the back dunes and far enough away from the salt spray and wind to allow the survival of trees and large shrubs.

Dune lake—freshwater lake that normally occurs within or at the edge of a dune forest.

Dune ridge—a raised mound of sand running parallel to the ocean.

Ecosystem—the various components, e.g., plants and animals, of a particular habitat.

Ectoparasite—a parasite that takes nourishment and lives outside its host.

Elytra—the modified first pair of wings on insects, usually hardened to protect the underlying membranous second pair of wings and the abdomen.

Emarginate—with a shallow notch at the apex.

Endemic—a native plant or animal that originated in an area.

Endoparasite—a parasite that takes nourishment and lives inside its host.

Entire—continuous and smooth, as a margin.

Ergot—elongated dark fungal fruiting bodies that parasitize grass kernels.

Evergreen—remaining green all year, through the dormant season.

Extrafloral nectary—nectar-producing organ located outside a flower.

Femur (*pl.* **femora**)—third segment of an insect's leg.

Flatworm—a primitive invertebrate with a simple body plan. Most are animal parasites, but a few are free-living predators.

Floret—a small flower, usually in a dense cluster.

Flower—reproductive plant structure bearing stamens, a pistil, and usually sepals and petals.

Flower fly—a fly of the family Syrphidae that visits flowers for pollen and nectar.

Flower spike—a stem containing rows of closely attached flowers.

Fluke—common name for a parasitic trematode larva.

Foliage—general term for all the vegetative portions of a plant.

Food chain—a food cycle starting with plants, then herbivores, then predators.

Foredune—area from the end of the strand to the first perennial herbaceous plants.

Frass—a mixture of insect feces and portions of the plant host.

Free-living—living in soil or water and not in living organisms.

Fruit—ripened ovary with associated floral parts.

Fungus (*pl.* **fungi**)—organism that lacks chlorophyll, reproduces by spores, and lives as a saprophyte or parasite.

Fuscous—a shade of dark or light brown.

Gall—abnormal plant growth caused by a foreign organism.

Gametocyst—reproductive stage in the life cycle of some protozoa.

Generalist—regarding food habits, an animal that can subsist on many different plants.

Genus—a group of species that share common morphological and genetic characters.

Giant cells—enlarged plant cells formed as a result of enzymes released by parasitic nematodes.

Gills—in a mushroom, a series of flat, spore-bearing structures.

Glaciation—movement of ice blocks (glaciers) that modify the present landscape.

Globose—spherical.

Gregarine—a protozoan parasite that forms cysts in invertebrates.

Grub—thick-bodied insect larva, usually of a beetle.

Guano—seabird droppings, usually found at the base of nesting sites.

Habitat—immediate surroundings of a plant or animal.

Hammock—mounds of sand formed by the wind.

Harvestman (*pl.* **harvestmen**)—an arachnid, also known as daddy longlegs.

Head capsule—the hardened portion of an insect's head.

Herb—a plant that lacks a firm woody structure and dies back to the ground.

Herbivore—an animal that eats plants.

Hermaphrodite—an individual that produces both sperm and eggs.

Hermaphroditism—reproduction with eggs and sperm in a single individual.

High tide zone—region on the beach where the tides reach their maximum level. This area changes depending on the strength of the tides.

Holdfast—a basal expansion of a stem that attaches to the substrate, as in many seaweeds.

Homotypic agglutination—the aggregation of different individuals of the same species for feeding and reproduction.

Honeydew—a sugary solution produced by sap-sucking insects, such as aphids.

Horsehair worms—long, dark, wiry worms that lack segments and appendages and that parasitize arthropods.

Host—an organism that is used as food by a parasite or pathogen.

Hypha (*pl.* **hyphae**)—a microscopic strand of a fungus.

Imago—adult insect.

Infection—the process of a parasite or pathogen invading a host.

Infective stage—the stage of a parasite that penetrates the body of a host.

Inquilinism—an association in which two organisms live together without harm or benefit to each other.

Instar—stage of an insect between molts.

Integument—outer body covering of an arthropod.

Intermediate host—an animal harboring the larval stage of a parasite that must reach yet another host to become mature.

Intertidal animal—one that lives in the zone between high and low tides.

Intertidal zone—land between the high and low tides.

Introduced plant—one that originated from another geographical area (not native).

Invasive species—an introduced and often noxious animal or plant that has adapted to the present habitat.

Invertebrate—animal lacking a backbone, such as an arthropod; includes insects.

Kelp—large seaweed.

Keystone species—a plant or animal species that supports a number of other species that depend on it for their survival.

Labium—lower portion of an insect's mouthparts.

Labrum—upper portion of an insect's mouthparts.

Larva (*pl.* **larvae**)—immature feeding stage between the egg and pupa, e.g., caterpillar.

Latex—a sticky white deposit emitted by plants.

Leaf-cutter bee—bee of the family Megachilidae that cuts out leaf sections for nest construction.

Legume—simple podlike fruit that splits open along the sides.

Life cycle—the various developmental stages in the life of an organism.

Longhorn beetle—a large beetle of the family Cerambycidae that has long antennae and legs.

Longitudinal—along the length of a structure, regarding body markings.

Lower dune—foredune.

Maggot—legless, soft, immature stage of a fly.

Mandibles—biting mouthpart structures.

Marsh—a low-lying wetland.

Microhabitat—the physical conditions occurring in a small, confined habitat such as under driftwood.

Microorganisms—microscopic organisms like single-celled fungi, bacteria, and protozoa.

Middune—region from the end of the foredune to the beginning of the perennial shrub region.

Midge—small fly with long, segmented antennae.

Miner—larval stage of an insect that develops within plant tissue.

Mite—a small spiderlike organism that normally has six legs when born but eight legs later in life.

Mollusks—invertebrate group that includes snails, slugs, and their relatives.

Molt—shedding the outermost skin layer.

Monophagous—feeding on one kind of food.

Morphology—structure or form of an organism.

Mushroom—general term for the spore-producing fruiting body of higher fungi.

Mutualism—an association between two organisms in which both benefit and neither is harmed.

Mycelium—a strand of hyphae, the vegetative structure of a fungus.

Mycorrhizal association—an association between a fungus and the root system of a higher plant.

Naiad—gill-breathing immature stage of certain aquatic insects.

Native plant—one that occurs naturally in a region and may have evolved there.

Necrosis—area of disease in plant or animal tissue.

Nectar—sugary deposit produced by a plant to attract insect pollinators or insect defenders.

Nectary—a nectar-secreting gland.

Nematode—a roundworm lacking body segments and appendages.

Nymph—terrestrial, air-breathing immature stage of some insects.

Ocellus (*pl.* **ocelli**)—simple eye, often in a group of two or three on an insect's head.

Ommatidium—a single unit of an insect's compound eye.

Omnivore—an organism that obtains nourishment from both animals and plants.

Opportunistic—taking advantage of the surrounding conditions.

Osmeterium—an eversible gland in caterpillars that releases defensive chemicals.

Ovary—the ovule or seed-producing part of a flower, usually positioned in or near the middle of the flower.

Ovipositor—apparatus in female insects used to deposit eggs. Can be modified as a "stinger" in some insects such as bees and yellow jackets.

Parasite—an organism that feeds in or on another organism (the host).

Parasitism—an association between two organisms in which one is harmed (usually by the removal of body tissues) and the other benefits.

Parasitoid—an insect that develops inside and eventually kills another insect.

Parthenogen—an individual that produces young from unfertilized eggs.

Parthenogenesis—reproduction without sperm.

Pathogen—a microorganism capable of causing disease in another organism.

Pearl mite—a parasitic mite whose females swell up into a shape resembling a pearl.

Pedicel—stem of one flower in a cluster.

Peduncle—stem of a flower cluster.

Perennial—a plant that survives year after year.

Petal—one unit of the inner floral envelope or corolla.

Petiole—leaf stalk.

Pinna (*pl.* **pinnae**)—fern leaf.

Pistil—female portion of a flower, comprising an ovary, style, and stigma.

Plant community—a plant together with its associated organisms. Can also mean a group of plants growing in the same habitat.

Plumose—feathery, as in some types of insect antennae.

Pod—a dry fruit containing seeds.

Pollen—male reproductive element of a flower.

Pollinator—an agent, usually an insect, that transfers pollen from one plant to another.

Pollinium—a small sac filled with pollen grains that becomes attached to pollinators.

Polyembrony—condition in which a single egg divides after being deposited, resulting in many offspring.

Posterior—the tail or tip portion.

Powdery mildew—a parasitic fungus that grows and produces patches of white or gray spores on host plants.

Predator—an organism that consumes more than one prey during its existence.

Prehensile—structure modified for holding.

Proboscis—tubelike modified mouthpart for taking up liquids.

Procumbent—lying flat, trailing, as some stems.

Progeny—the young of a mated pair.

Prolegs—"false" unjointed legs on the abdomen of some immature insects, especially caterpillars.

Pronotum—a hardened structure covering the prothorax.

Prostrate—lying flat on the ground.

Prothorax—body part behind an insect's head.

Protozoa—microscopic single-celled organisms.

Pubescence—a covering of hairs.

Pupa (*pl.* **pupae**)—a quiescent developmental stage between the larva and adult insect.

Puparium—case made by the hardening of the larval skin in many flies, where pupation occurs.

Pycnidia—minute fruiting structures of some plant-parasitic fungi.

Raptorial—legs modified for holding prey.

Ray florets—marginal, asymmetrical flowers in the flower heads of members of the sunflower family.

Reticulate—network-like.

Rhizobacteria—nitrogen-fixing bacteria that live in nodules on a plant's roots and convert nitrogen from the atmosphere into ammonia.

Rhizome—underground stem that produces aerial stems as it grows.

Rhizomorph—a miniature cord-like structure composed of fungal hyphae.

Rostrum—beak.

Roundworm—common name for a nematode.

Rugose—covered with wrinkles.

Runner—a long plant stem that grows along the ground surface. Also called a stolon.

Rush—a grasslike plant with round stems and small clusters of inconspicuous flowers.

Sand dune—a wide expanse of sand.

Sand hummocks—mounds or even small hills of sand created by wind action.

Saprophyte—an organism that obtains nourishment from dead organic matter.

Scales—small, flake-like structures on the surface of insects and plants.

Scarify—to scratch the surface of something, such as a seed to enhance germination.

Sclerotized—hardened portions of an insect's body wall.

Scutellum—small dorsal thoracic segment.

Seashore—area of land bordering the sea between the high- and low-water marks.

Sedge—a grass-like plant with triangular

stems and tightly formed flower heads that often grows in moist habitats.

Seed—a ripened ovule.

Seedpod—an enclosure containing seeds.

Seepage area—land saturated with water that drains away very slowly.

Sepal—floral element at the base of a flower, making up the calyx.

Seta (*pl.* **setae**)—sharp, stiff hair on the surface of an object.

Shore—land along the edge of a large body of water.

Shrub—a woody perennial plant that remains low and produces stems from the base.

Skeletonize—to strip away everything on a leaf except the veins.

Slime mold—a primitive fungus-like organism that has a slimy, flattened, mobile stage.

Slug—a terrestrial mollusk without a noticeable shell that secretes slime and feeds on plants.

Solitary—single or alone.

Sorus (*pl.* **sori**)—fruit dot or spore cluster on fern leaves.

Specialist—regarding food habits, an animal that feeds on only one plant or several.

Species—a group of interbreeding individuals with similar characteristics.

Spike—a simple unbranched row of many flower heads.

Spikelet—a series of florets forming a flower head, as in grasses.

Spine—sharp-pointed structure.

Spiracle—breathing pore on the side of an arthropods's abdomen.

Sporangium—a receptacle where asexual spores are formed.

Spore—a simple reproductive body, as found in fungi and ferns.

Spur—a tubular projection.

Stabilize—to keep sand from shifting under the influence of the wind.

Stamen—pollen-bearing organ of a flower.

Stem—the main leaf-bearing and flower-bearing axis of a plant.

Stigma—the part of a pistil that receives pollen.

Stolon—a stem that grows on the ground and can form roots.

Strand—the shore, beach, or intertidal zone.

Strand plant—a plant growing at, slightly under, or immediately above the high tide line.

Stria (*pl.* **striae**)—a groove on the surface of a structure, such as insect wing covers.

Stylet—a hollow, hardened tubular structure that is used for releasing enzymes and taking up plant juices, as in nematodes.

Symbiont—an organism that forms an association with a different organism.

Symbiosis—the living together of two separate individuals.

Tapeworm—a segmented parasitic worm that lives, as an adult, in a vertebrate's intestine.

Taproot—the main central root of many plants that stores food.

Tarn—a small, temporary body of water that usually dries by midsummer.

Tarsus (*pl.* **tarsi**)—terminal or fifth leg portion of an insect, normally composed of several discrete segments.

Tectonics—movement of the earth's plates that shapes the present landscape.

Tegmina—outer pair of wings of grasshopper-like insects.

Tendril—a string-like plant process, usually at the end of a stem, that twists around other plants for support.

Thorax—structural part of an insect behind the head where the legs and wings arise.

Tibia (*pl.* **tibiae**)—fourth leg segment of an insect, between the femur and tarsus.

Tidal flat—a low area adjacent to the sea that contains a mixture of sand and sediment.

Tide—the rise and fall in sea level at periodic intervals, roughly twice daily.

Transitional zone—area above normal high tides that is inundated only by extremely high tides.

Transverse—across the width, regarding color patterns on insects.

Trematode—a parasitic worm with a simple body plan that lives, as an adult, in vertebrates.

Trifoliate—with leaves divided in three parts.

Trochanter—second leg segment of an insect, between the coxa and femur.

Upper dune—back dune.

Urticating—stinging, as in nettles.

Vector—normally an insect, such as a mosquito, that transmits pathogens from one organism to another.

Veil—a fine membrane that connects the cap of a young mushroom to the stalk and is broken when the cap expands.

Venation—arrangement of veins in a leaf.

Venter—the underside or ventral side.

Vesicles—sacs.

Vesticles—sacs.

Vestiture—the degree of body covering by hairs or scales.

Whorl—three or more leaves arranged in a circle around a stem.

Wing covers—elytra or hard forewings on many adult insects.

Wireworm—the elongated, hard larva of a click beetle.

Wrack—decaying seaweed.

Zygomorphic flower—an asymmetrical flower.

SELECT BIBLIOGRAPHY

Arora, D. 1986. *Mushrooms Demystified: A Comprehensive Guide to the Fleshy Fungi.* Berkeley: Ten Speed Press.

Barbour , M. G., R. B. Craig, F. R. Drysdale, and M. T. Ghiselin. 1973. *Coastal Ecology: Bodega Head.* Berkeley: University of California Press.

Barry, W. J., and E. I. Schlinger, eds. 1977. *Inglenook Fen: A Study and Plan.* Sacramento: Department of Parks and Recreation, State of California.

Coombs, E. M., J. K. Clark, G. L. Piper, and A. F. Cofrancesco Jr., eds. 2004. *Biological Control of Invasive Plants in the United States.* Corvallis: Oregon State University Press.

Essig, E. O. 1958. *Insects and Mites of Western North America.* New York: MacMillan.

Haggard, P., and J. Haggard. 2006. *Insects of the Pacific Northwest.* Portland, OR: Timber Press.

Hatch, M. 1957–1971. *The Beetles of the Pacific Northwest.* 6 vols. Seattle: University of Washington Press.

Hickman, J. C., ed. 1996. *The Jepson Manual.* Berkeley: University of California Press.

Hitchcock, C. L., and A. Cronquist. 1973. *Flora of the Pacific Northwest.* Seattle: University of Washington Press.

Kaston, B. J. 1953. *How to Know the Spiders.* Dubuque, IA: W. C. Brown.

Meyers, S. C., Jaster, T., Mitchell, K. E., Hardison, L. K. (eds.) 2015. *Flora of Oregon. Volume 1: Pteridophytes, Gymnosperms, and Monocots.* Fort Worth: The Botanical Research Institute of Texas Press.

Miller, J. C., and P. C. Hammond. 2003. *Lepidoptera of the Pacific Northwest: Caterpillars and Adults.* Morgantown, WV: US Department of Agriculture, Forest Health Technology Enterprise Team.

Munz, P. A. 2003. *Introduction to Shore Wildflowers of California, Oregon, and Washington.* Rev. ed. California Natural History Guide No. 67. Berkeley: University of California Press.

Pickart, A. J., and J. O. Sawyer. 1998. *Ecology and Restoration of Northern California Coastal Dunes.* Sacramento: California Native Plant Society.

Pojar, J., and A. MacKinnon. 1994. *Plants of the Pacific Northwest Coast.* Redmond, WA: Lone Pine Publishing.

Powell, J. A., and C. L. Hogue. 1979. *California Insects.* Berkeley: University of California Press.

Powell, J. A., and P. A. Opler. 2009. *Moths of Western North America.* Berkeley: University of California Press.

Pyle, R. M. 1981. *National Audubon Society Field Guide to North American Butterflies.* New York: Alfred A. Knopf.

Wiedemann, A. M., L. R. J. Dennis, and F. H. Smith. 1999. *Plants of the Oregon Coastal Dunes.* Corvallis: Oregon State University Book Stores.

INDEX